Praise for
How to Have Difficult Conversations About Race

"Kwame has a powerful, yet tactful and empathetic approach to having difficult conversations about race, diversity, and inclusion—all topics that are now more paramount than ever . . . This book should be required reading for all people."
—Rebecca Zung, attorney, Amazon bestselling author of
***Negotiate Like YOU MATTER,* and high conflict negotiator**

"Kwame's relatable storytelling style, combined with his expertise in conflict negotiation, helps professionals across industries develop the tangible skills needed to build the confidence to engage in meaningful conversations about difficult topics, and the empathy needed to communicate across—and about—difference."
—Tiffany F. Southerland, Esq., career coach, speaker,
and host of the *How Does She Do It* podcast

HOW TO HAVE DIFFICULT CONVERSATIONS ABOUT RACE

Also by Kwame Christian

Finding Confidence in Conflict:
How to Negotiate Anything and Live Your Best Life

HOW TO HAVE DIFFICULT CONVERSATIONS ABOUT RACE

Practical Tools for Necessary Change in the Workplace and Beyond

KWAME CHRISTIAN

BenBella Books, Inc.
Dallas, TX

BenBella Books, Inc.
10440 N. Central Expressway
Suite 800
Dallas, TX 75231
benbellabooks.com
Send feedback to feedback@benbellabooks.com

BenBella is a federally registered trademark.

Printed in the United States of America
10 9 8 7 6 5 4 3 2 1

Library of Congress Control Number: 2022013475
ISBN 9781637741306 (hardcover)
ISBN 9781637741313 (electronic)

Editing by Leah Wilson and Alyn Wallace
Copyediting by James Fraleigh
Proofreading by Becky Maines and Jenny Bridges
Indexing by WordCo
Text design and composition by PerfecType, Nashville, TN
Cover design by Brian Lemus
Cover image © Shutterstock / teacept
Printed by Lake Book Manufacturing

Special discounts for bulk sales are available. Please contact bulkorders@benbellabooks.com.

To my family, thank you for the consistent love and support.
To my staff, thank you for helping to change the lives of millions.
To my clients and the people we serve, thank you for trusting us.

Whitney, Kai, and Dominic, thank you for your patience as I completed this project. After all the years of work, dedication, heartache, and pain that went into this, I hope that I made you all proud.

CONTENTS

Introduction   1

PART ONE   THE PROBLEM

Chapter One   Why It's Important to Talk About Race   17

Chapter Two   From Weakness to Strength: Creating a
                   Winning Mindset   27

Chapter Three Common Psychological Barriers   45

PART TWO   THE SOLUTION

Chapter Four   The Art of Strategy   77

Chapter Five   Mobilizing Compassionate Curiosity   113

Chapter Six   Avoid Common Mistakes   153

PART THREE TAKING ACTION

Chapter Seven How to Be an Advocate for Positive Change   181

Chapter Eight The Role of Difficult Conversations in
                   Equity Discussions   201

Appendix: The Advocate's Playbook: Handling Common
    Race-Related Scenarios at Work   213

Endnotes   221

Index   231

INTRODUCTION

The best things in life are on the other side of difficult conversations.
—The American Negotiation Institute's guiding principle

The topic of race and issues surrounding race have been coming up with ever-increasing frequency, and not just in the news and on social media. Conversations about race are also being held far more often in the workplace. As a society, we are more interested in racial equity than ever before—and that's a good thing. But conversations around race also tend to stir up strong opinions and powerful emotions, and unfortunately, most workplaces are woefully unprepared to manage the ensuing awkwardness and conflict. This jeopardizes workplace harmony and makes it harder for colleagues to collaborate and coexist. It also makes it more difficult for people who are trying to address issues of inclusion and belonging within the organization to persuade and influence others.

People who aren't used to talking about race and don't feel comfortable doing so—but find themselves in a position where they must—can be particularly ill-equipped for these conversations. Even people used to talking about race often find these conversations challenging. The potential for awkwardness and offense abounds. But so do the opportunities for creating connection and solving problems. While we've made great progress as a society in terms of race, equity, and justice, we still have a long way to go. To solve our remaining problems, we need to be able to talk to one another about them.

I'm the founder and CEO of the American Negotiation Institute (ANI), where we specialize in training and consulting in the realm of negotiation and conflict resolution. At ANI we believe the best things in life are on the other side of difficult conversations; it's our guiding principle. In addition to our negotiation and conflict resolution work, we also conduct diversity, equity, and inclusion (DEI) training and strategic consulting centered on creating connection through communication and cultural intelligence. We've had the opportunity to work with a wide variety of companies in different industries of every size that are experiencing DEI challenges. In the process, we've recognized an important issue: in the world of DEI, we're not just dealing with a knowledge gap, we're dealing with a skills gap. Yes, DEI programs should increase awareness and help people to understand diverse perspectives. However, these programs often miss a critical element: the ability to communicate respectfully and effectively about these serious issues.

That's what this book will teach you to do.

My goal isn't to teach you how to *think* about race. There are already a lot of great books on the history of race and racism, structural inequity, and more. But although these resources usually do a great job of outlining the challenges we face, they often overlook the difficulty of bridging the gap between problem and solution. *Both persuasive communication and conflict management play critical roles in whether meaningful change occurs in the workplace.* How can you solve problems if you don't have the skills to talk about them?

THE FIRST DIFFICULT CONVERSATION

In 2020, America went through yet another racial reckoning. The latest in a string of police-related deaths, the most notable of which were Breonna Taylor and George Floyd, played nonstop on the news. What made this reckoning different was that, because of the global COVID-19 pandemic and resulting lockdowns, we could do nothing else but watch story after heartbreaking story about police shootings, hate crimes against Asian Americans, and racial inequity. They were all over traditional and social media, making it seem like everybody was talking about race.

Everybody except me.

Before starting the American Negotiation Institute, and before the career I had in between as a business lawyer, I worked as a legal and policy analyst at the Kirwan Institute for the Study of Race and Ethnicity. There, I focused on matters concerning health equity and criminal justice. I would travel the country talking to health professionals about growing health inequities, what they could do to address them, and more specifically, how they could create persuasive arguments to overcome resistance to change from their leadership, local politicians, and community leaders. For example, one of my focuses in the world of health equity was infant mortality, defined as the death of an infant before their first birthday. Did you know that out of every 1,000 Black children born, 11 die? This is nearly double the rate for White infants, which is only 5.8 per 1,000 births.[1] There was no shortage of statistics like this, so helping health professionals address these persistent challenges is important and impactful work.

However, it felt like what I was doing was just a drop in the bucket. And all of those years I spent talking about inequity and injustice were psychologically and emotionally taxing. I was burnt out emotionally, spiritually, and intellectually, and was in desperate need of a change. So . . . I quit.

I ran as far away from anything that had to do with racial inequity as I could. For over a year, I stopped watching the news. If I saw a social media post with a political, inequality, or race-related message, I would unfollow the poster. I even went as far as to block my wife, Whitney, from time to time, because she's never been one to hold back when there's something on her mind, especially when it comes to matters of social justice.

Mental health–wise, shutting down and disconnecting from the world's problems was incredible! I never felt better. I was less stressed and much happier.

But even though I *felt* better, it didn't mean that everything *was* better.

Fast-forward to May 2020. By this time, after transitioning to the business world, I had built a career representing clients in legal negotiations, started to work as a mediator, and honed my conflict resolution skills. I had also found that my true passion was *teaching* negotiation skills. That passion led me to start ANI in 2016, and four years later, our team was growing quickly. I was enjoying the work and the positive impact it was having on the world. But, unfortunately, after the murders of Ahmaud Arbery, Breonna Taylor, and George Floyd, difficult conversations about race were becoming harder and harder to avoid.

On May 31, 2020, Whitney decided to have a difficult conversation with me. She said, "I know that you want to avoid this situation, Kwame. I know that you hate talking about this. But here's the thing—you always talk about how important it is for other people to engage in difficult conversations. How does it look if *you* are intentionally avoiding having difficult conversations?"

Damn.

I realized that avoiding the situation was not the same as choosing neutrality. My lack of engagement was causing harm. People were looking to me for guidance on how to have these difficult conversations about race, and I was silent—despite being *uniquely* qualified to address the issue. I'm a Black man in the field of negotiation and conflict resolution, which is rare. And my background in civil rights made me even more unique.

That's when I decided—reluctantly—to get involved.

I thought I'd just check the box and say I did my good deed, then go back into the shadows until these most recent incidents blew over. I'd have a little online event, maybe twenty or thirty people would show up, and then I'd be done. I posted about doing a virtual town hall on LinkedIn and titled it "How to Have Difficult Conversations About Race." To my surprise, the post went viral. We maxed out our online event capacity, with more than a thousand attendees from around the world.

I told them, "I'm not going to tell you how to think about race, I'm going to show you *how to talk about race.*" I provided simple and practical tools for having these difficult conversations that people could immediately put into action. Attendees discovered that they could have these conversations in a way that was constructive, not destructive.

Following a brief presentation, I promised the attendees that I would stay as long as they needed and answer questions. I answered the last question three hours later. Even though I was the person presenting, the audience taught me something very important: people are hungry for this information. They want to learn how to communicate and connect on this sensitive issue. It's my hope that this book will teach you how to do just that.

THE GOAL AND SCOPE OF THIS BOOK

Maybe you've thought or heard someone else explain their hesitance to talk about race like this:

> *I know we have some serious problems regarding race to address in our workplace and in our society. But when I try to tell people about it and share the data, they just don't get it. It's so frustrating.*

> *Everybody here is afraid to talk about our company's challenges around race. I can't get people to engage. It makes it hard for me to solve the problem if we can't even talk about the problem.*

> *I'm a leader in my organization and I worked hard to earn the position that I have. I got here because I'm good at what I do. I don't want to have these conversations about race because they make me feel uncomfortable, but they are becoming harder and harder to avoid.*

> *I'm one of the youngest people in our organization. The folks in the older generation don't seem to see any issues, but I do. I want to do something, but I'm afraid of being punished for stepping out of line.*

I just experienced or witnessed a microaggression at work. The person who did it doesn't seem to think it's a problem, but it's really interfering with my or someone else's work experience, and I don't know what to say or how to say it.

I'm White and I want to be an ally, but talking about this is awkward. I don't want to say something wrong and be labeled a racist or accused of not staying in my lane, so I stay quiet. But sometimes when I stay quiet, I get accused of being racist. I feel like I'm in a lose-lose situation. When should I speak up, and what do I say?

So many of the reasons people don't have conversations about race come down to fear:

- the fear of being canceled or labeled a racist
- the fear of being misunderstood
- the fear of offending somebody
- the fear of being uncomfortable

Even finding the right words to use for having conversations about race feels hazardous. For example, is it:

- Hispanic or Latino/a or Latinx?
- White or Caucasian?
- Black or African American?
- Native American or American Indian or Indigenous American?
- Indian or South Asian?
- Nonwhite or people of color (POC) or Black, Indigenous, and people of color (BIPOC)?

Terms that were once generally considered acceptable are now considered politically incorrect, which can leave you feeling, as one person put it, "on your toes because you never know what to say."[2] It's easy to get overwhelmed before even starting the conversation—like, no matter what terminology you choose, you're going to offend someone.

It's hard for me, too. Finding the right terminology to use in this book felt like such a daunting task that I ended up asking my LinkedIn tribe for help. (Using their advice, I've chosen to be as specific as I can, where I can, particularly thanks to the guidance of Marisa Tatum, director of communications at Strategic Diversity Partners: "I don't particularly care for the current acronyms. The groups are so varied, it seems nonsensical to lump them together in most cases. I try to be as specific as possible when I can." Otherwise, I've chosen to use BIPOC.)

Sometimes we're just not sure what to say or how to say it. Most of us haven't been trained in how to have difficult conversations in general, so how can we assume that we know how to have difficult conversations about race? The goal of this book is to give you that training, and with it the confidence and skills necessary to have these conversations in a way that is productive and not destructive.

These skills can help you communicate more effectively everywhere, but I've chosen to focus on the workplace for three main reasons. First, given my work with ANI conducting negotiation and conflict resolution workshops for businesses, it's a context that I know well. Second, the challenges associated with these difficult conversations about race are particularly impeding inclusion and belonging at work. Third, we spend a lot of time at work; moreover, for most of us, it's our primary source of income and social status. Because of this, I believe that if we are able to overcome race-related challenges and create positive change in our workplaces, it will generate positive momentum that can help us to overcome race-related challenges and create positive change in our society as a whole.

It's nearly impossible to be an effective leader in today's multicultural workplace without understanding how to engage in difficult conversations about race or communicate effectively with people whose lived experiences differ from yours. Change in your organization, like change in society, takes collective action. However, conversation *must* come before action. If there's a change you want to make in your organization, unless you have the power to make it unilaterally, you first have to persuade others of the need for change, then talk through how best to achieve it. What good is knowing what needs to happen if you're unable to persuade people of it? How can a group of individuals coordinate their collective efforts to solve a problem without talking about it first?

Effective communication is one of the most important—yet often overlooked—parts of the process of creating positive change. If you try to take action *before* laying a strong foundation with these difficult conversations, you are less likely to garner the political capital necessary to put your plan into action, and more likely to alienate potential allies and stakeholders. You can end up doing more harm to your cause than good.

This can be particularly complex in a multigenerational office environment. Older professionals have largely been socialized to believe that conversations about race are impolite and inappropriate for the workplace, whereas the younger generation is more likely to believe that unapologetic political and social expression is a crucial part of their authentic identity. One of the tenets of inclusion is allowing people to bring their whole selves to work. Your whole self also includes how you think about sensitive topics like race. Younger professionals also tend to want to work at organizations that demonstrate a value-driven mentality.

All of this has put leaders in a very challenging position. There is no "safe" solution here; avoidance isn't the answer. You're going to need to have these conversations at some point, so you might as well learn how to have them in a way that is constructive and beneficial for your business. And call me a radical, but I believe that our workplaces should be a place of enjoyment and improvement. On average we spend approximately thirteen full years of our lives at work (assuming fifty years of employment).[3] That's a significant amount of time spent doing anything, especially given that, over an average lifetime, we spend only 328 *days* socializing with friends.[4] Thus, any place you spend that much time should be a place where you feel appreciated, valued, and accepted. When it comes to improving your organization, you should always seek ways to make your workplace better, as a leader or an employee. Having difficult conversations about race is an important way of doing that.

A CONSISTENT FRAMEWORK FOR SUCCESS

I'm assuming you're here because conversations about race have been challenging for you, but you want to improve because you believe these conversations matter. We don't have these conversations because they're easy. *We have them because they're necessary and worth it.*

You also want to be more *effective* in these conversations. What does it mean to have an "effective" conversation on the topic of race? I believe that, as with any communication, it's critical to be outcome oriented, whether the desired outcome is to influence, persuade, or simply escape the conversation respectfully without damaging the relationship. Once you clearly understand what it is that you're trying to accomplish, you can then use the appropriate approach to achieve your goals.

This, of course, is easier said than done. And when it comes to talking about race, there is no one-size-fits-all solution or technique for every situation. Despite some similarities across organizations, each one has specific challenges. The context, history, and structures of your organization are unique, so the solutions to your challenges and the outcomes you're looking for will likely be unique as well.

However, here's something important to understand: even though every situation is unique, predictable patterns of thought and behavior will be involved. That's what I love about psychology. It can bring order to the chaos of these complicated human interactions.

Different people have different goals in these conversations and different reasons for engaging. Some just want to share what's on their minds; some are confused and want to learn; some want to create positive change within their organizations. This variety of reasons for engaging can be overwhelming. But the strategy and mindset necessary to succeed across these conversations are roughly the same. Of course, we'll need to adjust slightly depending on the situation and the desired outcome, but the underlying framework won't vary much. If you're able to absorb and enact a few simple principles, you'll start to see these conversations as opportunities to connect, not threats to avoid.

HOW TO USE THIS BOOK TO DO BETTER AND BE BETTER (WHAT TO EXPECT FROM THIS BOOK)

This book gives you realistic and reliable tools that work—not theory. I don't want you to flounder in a perpetual state of deep thought. I want you to finish reading this book and take action.

After reading this book, you will have:

1. practical skills to put into action in these conversations.
2. more confidence when having these conversations.
3. less fear and pressure during these conversations.

I want you to be able to rely on your skills, not your hopes. Many times, when people encounter a problem, they use what I call a "hope-based" strategy. Instead of actually saying or doing something to create the reality they desire, they sit back passively and just hope that things will get better on their own. But here's the problem: hope is not a strategy. You need to be proactive.

Let's say you're a leader in your organization and you recognize that the retention rates for high-performing BIPOC within your organization are significantly lower than average. Upon further investigation, you realize that most of your BIPOC colleagues who left said that they "didn't feel as though they belonged." Your remaining BIPOC colleagues echo this sentiment. A hope-based strategy would lead you to say to yourself, "I hope our organization changes its culture in order to become more inclusive," without taking further action. When you don't know what you can or should say to create positive change in situations like these, you're much more likely to fall back on hope. One of my goals with this book is to empower you with the mindset and skill set you need to feel more confident having these conversations, so you can stop simply relying on hope and instead rely on your ability to create positive change.

Disclaimer: You aren't going to agree with everything you read in this book. That's okay. Consider this text more as a toolbox than a rigid step-by-step guide. Take what you like and leave what does not work for you. I don't want you to communicate like Kwame; I want you to communicate like you. Think about how you can use these tools to create a personal persuasive style that is both authentic and effective.

All I ask is that you start to become more outcome oriented and begin to think critically about how you can have these conversations in a way that boosts your odds of getting the results you want. By being proactive instead of reactive, you can profoundly improve the state of your circumstances and your relationships, both at work and beyond.

This book was designed by a democratic process. Each chapter arose from the questions and concerns of the thousands of people who have attended our trainings, as well as questions from my followers on LinkedIn and students in my LinkedIn Learning courses. There are a lot of things that I want to talk about, but I want to narrow our focus to talk about the things that matter most to you.

First, we'll address the challenges you'll face in these conversations, beginning with a deeper dive into our internal barriers to even initiating these conversations. You can't overcome challenges if you don't see or understand them. We'll also look at psychological obstacles that are likely to arise *during* these conversations, both in ourselves and others, and how to address them. We often overlook our own roles in these difficult conversations, in favor of focusing on external forces. We are quick to blame others or blame culture, but we rarely blame ourselves. When these difficult conversations get off track, we rarely take the time to consider how we contributed to the situation. This is a disempowering stance.

Next, we'll discuss strategy—how to approach these conversations for maximum impact—and move into the core of my methodology for handling these difficult conversations: the Compassionate Curiosity framework. This framework is designed for conflict resolution generally but is especially useful in difficult conversations about race. My approach is not based on helping you to "win" or persuade, per se (although persuasion is often a natural byproduct of this approach); it's focused on understanding, because people are usually unwilling to change their hearts and minds if they don't believe that you understand where they're coming from. This is the foundation for constructive conversations. We'll also take a moment to discuss common mistakes that take us further away from our goals.

Finally, we'll wrap up with advocacy and allyship. Now that we have these foundational conversational skills, we'll discuss how you can use the strategies from this book to create positive change in your organization.

To assist you in developing your voice within difficult conversations, I've included a series of discussion questions at the end of each chapter. If you are reading this book with friends, family, or colleagues—as part of a book club, in an organization-wide initiative, or within an employee resource group, for example—you can use these questions to share your thoughts in a safe place and practice using the communication techniques from this book. If you are reading solo, consider journaling the answers and revisiting what you've written once you've finished the book; your answers might change. Having a written baseline can assist in your personal growth or reveal areas of your communication style that need further attention.

I want this book to spark discussion. I'm not perfect, and your feedback, whether you agree or disagree, is ultimately beneficial; the more conversations we have about how to have constructive conversations on the topic of race, the better we'll all get at approaching these crucial discussions.

Conversations about race are some of the most difficult conversations you're going to have in your professional life. However, if you are able to navigate them well, the impact can change your relationships, your life—even the world.

Thank you for taking this journey with me. I'm excited for you to be here. Let's get started!

DISCUSSION QUESTIONS

- Why are you reading this book?
- Finish this sentence: After reading this book, I want to be able to . . .
- What changes for you if you can achieve this goal?
- What changes in your environment (your workplace, family, or community) if you are able to achieve this goal?
- What are the risks if you *do not* take action?

PART ONE

The Problem

CHAPTER ONE

WHY IT'S IMPORTANT TO TALK ABOUT RACE

If you picked this book up for yourself, you likely think it's a given that we should talk about race at work—or that it's inevitable and you want to be prepared. But you might find that your colleagues don't share those sentiments. If you're unable to articulate why it's important to have these conversations, it's unlikely that you'll be able to persuade other people to engage.

There are lots of reasons why we should talk about race in the workplace. When I ask business leaders and other professionals why they believe we should have these conversations, their responses are consistent but unsatisfying. They usually respond with some version of the following:

- It's unavoidable. Race is going to come up, so you might as well know how to talk about it.
- If we don't practice these conversations, we won't get better at them.
- We can't solve problems if we can't talk about them.
- Studies show that diversity is good for business.

Although I don't necessarily disagree with any of these answers, none of them gets to the core rationale for having these conversations. To me, the reason we should be talking about race at work comes down to one simple word: *care*.

One of the most hurtful things you can say to someone is "I don't care." In the words of Holocaust survivor and writer Elie Wiesel, "The opposite of love is not hate, it's indifference." In any relationship, whether business or personal, the people involved need to know that their care is reciprocated. Talking to people about the things that are important to them is one of the easiest ways to show you care. Your workplace consists of a system of interconnected relationships. We have difficult conversations at work, whether about race or anything else, because we care about those relationships.

I know there are going to be people reading this who don't like to talk about race in the workplace and who are saying, "I *do* care about my colleagues, and the relationships I have with them! It's not fair for you to say that I don't." And I'm sure you do! But if you care, and you're still not having these conversations, it means that you care *more* about something else.

For example, I care about hanging out with my friends. But after I got married and had kids, I cared *more* about spending time with my family—and, as a result, the time that I spent with my friends decreased. Something else took priority.

One of the major goals of the human brain is the conservation of energy. Although the brain only comprises 2 percent of your body mass, it uses up to 20 percent of the body's energy—more than any other organ.[1] Because of this, it is constantly looking for ways to use less energy. It will therefore choose the easiest option (unless it has a particularly good reason not to).

Conversations about race require a lot of time and effort, two things that are in short supply in the workplace. This makes avoidance one of the natural cognitive responses to discussions centered around sensitive topics. The problem is that any kind of progress—whether interpersonal, professional, or societal—requires effort, often a significant amount. Similarly, progress often requires time spent in discomfort—something that taxes the brain.

So it's not that people who don't talk about race don't care about others or race-related issues. It's that they are, often unknowingly, prioritizing the conservation of energy and comfort.

This response is understandable. It is challenging for those who do not feel the impact of race-related issues in the workplace to fully appreciate those issues and why these conversations are so important. *This is not an indictment of their morality. It's a recognition of their humanity.* It also gives us the key to convincing avoiders to engage in conversations about race: helping them understand why the effort and discomfort are worth it. That means shifting their focus to the benefits of having these conversations and the reality that, in many cases, showing that you care means leaning into these discussions about race.

So what is it that we care about that explains why difficult conversations about race are necessary, especially at work?

1. We care about our colleagues and our relationships with them.
2. We care about fairness.
3. We care about progress.

WE CARE ABOUT OUR COLLEAGUES AND OUR RELATIONSHIPS WITH THEM

In 2020, I was invited to be on a Dutch show to discuss how to talk about race. The host explained that, in the Netherlands, he was taught to be color blind and believed that this approach was the solution to a lot of the racial problems in society. This is something I've heard time and time again, and I believe in most instances it comes from a good place—but the approach is often inadequate for a number of reasons. So I decided to respectfully challenge him by saying, "You're a father. How would you feel if I said I don't see your son?"

His identity as a father was something he was proud of—something that was important to him. How hurtful would it be for me to deny that part of him? To ignore his identity as if it were something shameful? You can't have a meaningful relationship with someone while denying an integral part of their identity.

Who we are is made up of our collection of life experiences. Race, ethnicity, and culture not only have a profound impact on how we engage with the world, but also on how the world engages with us. If we care about the relationships we have with our colleagues at work and want those relationships to grow stronger, we have to recognize and accept our differences, and the varying life experiences that led to them.

One of the most beautiful things about working in a multicultural workplace is that we can avail ourselves of a diversity of perspectives that together enrich our ability to analyze, strategize, problem-solve, and take advantage of opportunities. When we mute conversations about race, we make it exponentially difficult to do this. If anyone feels their ability to express themselves authentically is stymied, then we collectively miss out on a depth and richness of conversation that can spark creative ingenuity.

Of course, these differences in perspective can lead to misunderstandings and disagreements, and that's okay. All relationships, personal or professional, have challenges; this is the nature of human interaction. But when these challenges arise, especially around something as integral to our identities as race, we need to address them in some capacity. Even if you're ultimately unable to solve the problem, the relationship still benefits because we acknowledged the problem and communicated respectfully about it. However, if you instead respond with inaction or avoidance, people will question whether you care, which has implications not only for the other person's feelings about their role in the company, but also for the quality of your personal relationship.

Relationships go both ways, and caring about a relationship entails caring about the well-being of *everyone* in the relationship—including yourself. When problems arise, we engage in difficult conversations because, as Zabeen Mirza—negotiation expert, founder of Jobs.mom, and host of the Moms at Work podcast—explains, they're organic opportunities to engage in self-advocacy. By having them, we:

1. set boundaries and expectations,
2. help others to understand exactly what we need and what our requirements are, and
3. communicate what kind of support we need in order to perform effectively.

These things don't just benefit us. They ultimately benefit the relationship, because you are coaching people on how you want to be treated. This gives them an opportunity to adjust, which is important because they may not even know that adjustments should be made.

The more we communicate, the better we understand ourselves and one another. While conversations about sensitive issues like race are often seen as risky, when done appropriately, they can be sources of deeper connection and mutual understanding—*even if we ultimately don't agree.*

Here's what it really comes down to: when you care about your colleagues and believe that they care about you, from time to time you will have to have difficult conversations on a number of topics, including race. How can you show that you care about someone if you are unwilling or unable to speak to their fundamental emotional needs? How can you show somebody you care if you won't talk about things that are important to them? How can you show somebody you care if you're unwilling to address and acknowledge the challenges they face? You can't have a meaningful relationship with someone if you can't prove to the person that you care.

WE CARE ABOUT FAIRNESS

Fairness is something we as human beings care about deeply. Researchers have documented (and parents around the world can attest) that children as young as two years old demonstrate clear appreciation of and sensitivity to fairness.[2] Not surprisingly, conversations about what is, or is not, considered fair are constantly happening in the workplace. Whether regarding pay, access to opportunity, preferential treatment, or issues of inclusion and belonging, discussions about fairness as it relates to race have arisen with ever-increasing frequency.

We want our workplaces to be fair, and we care about making that happen. But we often make the mistake of thinking about fairness as a simple fact. We like to believe that things are either fair or unfair and that we can come to that conclusion objectively. However, whether we perceive something as fair is based on our unique perspective. It's easy to notice unfairness when you believe that you are the one being treated unfairly. However, if you have the luxury of not being treated unfairly—or being treated preferentially—it can be much harder to see the unfair treatment of others. Thus, whether you perceive something as fair is largely based on whether you hold the advantage.

Historically speaking, it is usually BIPOC employees who find themselves in a disadvantaged position in the workplace. As such, often they are both on the receiving end of unfair treatment and also bear the burden of raising awareness of it.

The leadership of most companies today recognizes the need for greater racial equity in the workplace along with the need for a workplace culture that makes all members of the team feel as though they are accepted and belong. The challenge is determining any unique barriers to equity and inclusion in a particular company, and how to address them—and it's impossible for companies to conduct these kinds of analyses *without* having difficult conversations about race. The skills to negotiate, manage conflict, and reconcile differences while being respectful, empathetic, and persuasive are essential to this process. If we care about fairness, we need to have these conversations, and we're going to have to learn how to have them effectively.

WE CARE ABOUT PROGRESS

Imagine this scene at a political rally. A charismatic politician stands up and yells, "If you elect me, I promise you that things will be no better than before!" And the crowd goes wild, chanting, "Stag-na-tion! Stag-na-tion!"

No political candidate runs on the status quo. Even incumbents say that they are going to try to do better than before. Why? The human desire for progress.

In his book *Affective Neuroscience*, neuroscientist Jaak Panksepp outlines seven core instincts: anger, fear, panic-grief, maternal care, pleasure/lust, play—and seeking. The seeking instinct involves the emotions that encourage people to explore for resources, which was critical to early humans' survival.[3] The curiosity and desire for *more* that come with it extend beyond the search for food to the abstract and are responsible for our never-ending quest for development as people. We want to be better than before—as individuals, and as a society.

In the workplace, *being better* can mean a lot of different things. To take one example: in our increasingly multicultural and multiracial workplaces, BIPOC employees still feel less comfortable than their White counterparts. According to a 2021 study from COQUAL's research report *Equity at Work: Fulfilling Its Promise Through Process*, over 35 percent of African American and Latinx employees, as well as 45 percent of Asian employees, believe that they need to "compromise their authenticity" in order to conform and be accepted in the workplace.[4] This pressure leads to diminished work performance and higher chances that BIPOC employees will leave in search of a more inclusive culture. *Being better* here means creating an office culture atmosphere where people feel comfortable expressing themselves openly and authentically—where people feel like they belong.

Culture is created by the collective of individuals within a space. If you want a more positive and inclusive culture, then you have to start, as a company, by embracing and encouraging meaningful conversations about race, while giving people the skills to manage these conversations in a way that brings them together rather than pushing them further apart. This also provides a foundation for progress in other areas. For your employees to work together effectively to identify and solve problems within the organization, you need them to feel like a team.

CONFLICT IS A NATURAL PART OF PROGRESS

We recently pitched a DEI assessment and strategic plan to a large company. During the last round of interviews, I said to the company's leadership team, "My biggest concern for you is that you'll create a perfect strategic plan, but the implementation of that plan will actually create *more* problems for your office."

"Wait, what do you mean?" they asked.

"You're looking for someone to conduct an assessment and use that data to create a strategic plan, right?"

"Yes."

"Well, let me tell you a secret. All of the companies you're considering can do that. Analyzing data and creating a plan is the easiest part. The problem is that there will be conflict before, during, and after the implementation of the plan. Have any of the other firms you're talking to provided you with a strategy to address this inevitable conflict?"

After an awkward silence, they said, "No."

"Well, regardless of who you end up going with, remember this: it doesn't matter how good your plan is if you're unable to execute due to inability to manage conflict. You would just be paying a lot of money to create more problems."

One of the main reasons it can be so challenging to create real change in the workplace is that a solution is only as good as your ability to persuade the people within your organization to implement it.

There's a big difference between passion and persuasion. That's why the skills of negotiation, conflict management, and effective communication are so critical to the process of creating positive change. Skillfully having difficult conversations is how you manage that inevitable conflict. And remember, difficult conversations are also how you show you care: about your colleagues, about fairness, and about progress. Absent proof of that care, you can't truly create change.

We've established why these conversations are so important—why we need to have them, even though they're hard. Next, let's look at what we can do to make them more manageable, starting with getting a better understanding of the psychological barriers, in ourselves and others, that make these conversations so challenging.

DISCUSSION QUESTIONS

- What do you care about in your workplace that makes difficult conversations about race necessary?
- What difficult conversations about race are currently being avoided in your workplace (by you or others), or have been avoided in the past?
- Do changes need to be made in your workplace? If so, what are some potential points of conflict that may arise?

CHAPTER
TWO

FROM WEAKNESS TO STRENGTH: CREATING A WINNING MINDSET

My parents are Caribbean immigrants. My father is from Dominica and my mother is from Guyana. When I was three years old, my family moved from Wilmington, Delaware, to Tiffin, Ohio. In case you're unfamiliar with the demographics of Tiffin, Ohio: of the 18,604 people who lived there at the time, 18,112 were White.[1] To add to this, not only was I the only Black kid in my school, but I also had a strong Caribbean accent that made me stand out even more.

One of my earliest memories is of recess one day in first grade. Looking for some friends to play with, I went up to a group of kids, who were gathered around talking, and asked if I could join them. They said no. So I went to another group of kids, who were playing kickball, and asked if I could play with them. They said no, too. I spent the entire recess looking, but nobody wanted to play with me. Eventually, the bell rang and everyone ran inside. And as hard as I tried, I couldn't keep it together. I started bawling. To this day, I have never felt more alone or humiliated.

That day in first grade is the first memory I have of feeling rejected for my race, my culture, and my identity.

In my first book, *Finding Confidence in Conflict*, I talked about how this incident impacted how I handled difficult conversations *in general* and what it took to become an assertive communicator. In my efforts to make friends and to prevent myself from feeling like I did that day on the playground, I became a people pleaser, often feeling like I couldn't stand up for myself. I became deathly terrified of conflict, because I didn't want to risk losing the friends I had worked so hard to get, and I didn't want to stand out more by disagreeing. But it's not hard to imagine how that day impacted me in difficult conversations about race, too.

In psychology, the term *racial trauma* describes a form of "race-based stress" in reaction to "perceived experiences of racial discrimination." These experiences "may include threats of harm and injury, humiliating and shaming events, and witnessing racial discrimination" toward other people who share the same racial identity.[2] These experiences not only impact our mental health—they also can have a lifelong impact on how we approach and experience sensitive conversations about race.

It's important to note that my experiences and relationships while in Tiffin were *overwhelmingly positive*. I made and still have great friends there, and I appreciate the childhood that we had. So why does that specific recess stand out? One of the most frustrating idiosyncrasies of the human mind is that it is primed to focus on the negative. It's easier for us to remember bad memories than good ones. Scientists postulate that this is because it's important for us to remember negative events for survival purposes. Remembering the bad things—a berry that made us sick, a person who betrays us—helps us protect ourselves.[3] That means that even when instances of racial trauma are infrequent, they still have a profound effect on your psyche.

Many of us are carrying some kind of emotional baggage as it relates to the topic of race in society. Conversations about race are almost always about more than just the issue at hand, because we are often haunted by pain from the past. It's like a wound that never heals; the pain stays fresh even though the event occurred long ago.

Many of us have had past discussions about race that didn't go as well as we would have liked—maybe because of an offensive comment that was made, or because of our or the other person's inability to empathize—and we carry that baggage into our conversations as well. A friend of mine named Melanie is a Black woman operating at the highest level within her company. Because of the small number of Black women in executive-level positions, during discussions about human relations issues, she is often the only person of color in the room. Even though Melanie's role has nothing to do with diversity and inclusion, as the only POC at the table she is often the only advocate for those issues.

A number of her BIPOC colleagues in the company confided in her about their frustrations with the company culture. They didn't feel as though it was inclusive enough, and a number of them planned to leave. So Melanie decided to bring it up to the company leaders in the next meeting. Unfortunately, the conversation went poorly. The chairman of the board shut her down immediately. "Listen," he said, "this is a business. If people are going to be overly sensitive, they can go work in a nonprofit. But if they want to work here, they are going to have to develop thicker skin. Their hypersensitivity isn't our problem, and I think we should use the remainder of the meeting to focus on legitimate business issues."

Melanie felt belittled and humiliated. She felt that her concerns, and those of her colleagues, were not being taken seriously. What was worse, after the meeting, no one said anything about the interaction—it was like everyone pretended it didn't happen. The situation left Melanie feeling hopeless. "They act like they want diverse voices," Melanie told me, "but then when we speak up, we're silenced and dismissed. What is the point? If I say anything, I am just going to be labeled as the 'angry Black woman.' It's time to start polishing the résumé."

Or consider the story of James, a White former firefighter who, after retirement, dedicated his life to ministry, leading mission trips to Ghana with his suburban church. In the summer of 2020, the church decided to start a book club to get a better understanding of the race-related challenges in America. They were brainstorming what to read with the group when a few of the members suggested a book that James and a large portion of the congregation found to be problematic.

James told the group that, although he agreed with the importance of the topic, he didn't feel comfortable with the choice of book. While it made several insightful points, he thought it was "unnecessarily offensive and seemed to imply that all White people were racist." Then he added, "I think our congregation would benefit from this book club, but there are hundreds of great books on this topic. Maybe we should pick one that's less controversial."

This didn't go over well with some of the members in attendance. They were livid. They accused him of being unwilling to wrestle with the harsh realities of race in America.

"Whoa! Hold on a second," he responded. "I am more than willing to wrestle with these realities. I think our church *needs* this book club. I'm just saying I think some of the premises of this book are unfounded and needlessly offensive in a way that will work against what we're trying to accomplish. There are other great options. Why does it need to be this particular book?"

The book's most vocal proponent didn't even look at James when they turned to the rest of the group and said, "This is the kind of fragility and defensiveness that I've been talking about. These people who act nice on the surface are the biggest problem because they tacitly perpetuate racism by protecting themselves from different perspectives."

James was flabbergasted. He wanted to argue, but he was afraid to make matters worse. So he backed down and didn't say anything else for the rest of the meeting.

When he shared the story with me, he said, frustrated, "It's a lose-lose situation. It's like they twist my words so that if I don't wholeheartedly agree with everything they say, then I'm automatically labeled a racist. And then if I defend myself, I'm both 'fragile' *and* a 'racist.' How is this helping anything? I don't even feel comfortable being involved anymore because it feels like no matter what I try to contribute, I'm wrong."

A conversation about race that goes wrong is like a hot stove—you only need to be burned once, or maybe twice, before you learn to stay away. To be able to make progress, we need to learn how to have difficult conversations despite old wounds, and without letting past experiences get in the way of addressing the problem at hand. We have to change our expectations and our mindset: about what constitutes success, about our own power, and more.

CONFLICT IS AN OPPORTUNITY FOR PROGRESS

The first step is to change how we think about these conversations—from a source of past (and potential future) trauma to an opportunity for progress. Your perspective impacts the way you engage. Your mind is creative; whatever you go into these conversations expecting, your mind will help you find it.

How are you defining conflict? When you see conflict as something bad, you'll dwell on the reasons a particular conflict or conversation is bad. If you see conflict as something scary, then you'll find reasons to be scared. If you view conflict negatively, you find reasons not to engage.

People often conflate conflict with combat, but combat is an altercation where the goal is to inflict more damage than you sustain. If you view conflict as combat, then not only will you be trying to inflict damage in these conversations, but you will also be scared of being hurt. On the other hand, if you see conflict as an opportunity, you'll be looking for opportunities— which can motivate you to push past your discomfort.

Making this shift in how we see difficult conversations means developing opportunity-based thinking. With this type of thinking, you analyze a situation and look for the opportunities it provides. Conflict provides us with the opportunity to:

- create positive change.
- connect with and learn about others.
- learn about ourselves.
- strengthen and maintain valuable relationships.

- promote equity.
- solve problems.
- avoid undesirable outcomes.
- improve our skill, ability, and poise in difficult conversations.

When we see conflict as an opportunity rather than combat, it allows us to navigate difficult conversations without the threat of inevitable pain. If we respect that our conversation partner currently sees the situation one way, while we see the situation another way, we can take advantage of the conflict to learn about the other person's emotional challenges, substantive challenges, and goals, and share our own. If you start with this foundation, you position yourself to work with the other person to create an outcome acceptable to both parties.

Every social interaction provides us with a strategic opportunity to accomplish our long-term goals. But sometimes it's difficult to see the opportunities available in these interactions, especially if we aren't thinking clearly because of stress. In these cases, challenge yourself to finish this sentence: "This conversation is an opportunity to . . ."

This doesn't mean that every conflict is worth your time. Asking yourself, "What is the point of this conversation?" can be an eye-opening exercise. When you answer this question, you might find that your only goal is to make somebody feel bad or to show that you are right. You might recognize that your goal is more emotional than rational and that having the conversation may end up causing more harm than good.

One of our trainers at ANI, Veronica Cravener, focuses on conflict resolution and has conducted hundreds of mediations. One of the things she always tells participants is that "disagreement is part of the process." She's found that when people expect that the other side won't automatically agree, they are more resilient in the face of resistance. You should do the same for yourself. Recognize that the person you're talking to won't always agree with you, and that's okay. It doesn't mean the conversation was a failure. And there are ways to benefit from even the most seemingly frustrating conversation.

Let's say that you are involved in a particularly challenging conversation where emotions are running high. The best-case scenario might not be to get them to change their worldview and behavior in just one interaction. Instead, it might be for you to end the conversation while:

- not damaging your relationship.
- getting as much information as possible to understand your conversation partner's perspective.
- scheduling a follow-up conversation where achieving your goal might be more likely.

When we strategically break a conversation into smaller pieces, each of those pieces is called a micro-negotiation. Using micro-negotiations still accomplishes something valuable, so don't be afraid to use an incremental approach. The opportunity doesn't end with the conversation unless you let it. Keep trying. Persistence is one of the most important parts of the persuasive process.

Difficult conversations can and should be transformational—not only for the person you are talking to but also for yourself. Seeing any transformation, no matter how small, is a win. And if you view difficult conversations through this lens—as opportunity rather than combat, and as a chance to make incremental progress—they'll feel less daunting, and easier to approach.

BINARY THINKING

Seeing an individual conversation as either a total success or a complete failure is a form of *binary thinking*. In life, there are few absolutes. There are very few times when people are either 100 percent good or 100 percent bad. It is also rare that ideas are either 100 percent good or 100 percent bad. It is unicorn-rare that we are 100 percent successful or 100 percent a failure in any of our endeavors.

When we forget that change happens incrementally and that every bit of forward movement is a success, we become frustrated and give up too soon. Improvement takes time. Therefore, we need to create more manageable milestones for ourselves. For example, success might be having a conversation with a limited scope where you show that you care and you're willing to listen. This might be the catalyst for their willingness to reciprocate in the next conversation and give meaningful consideration to your perspective. Focusing on small wins will yield better long-term results.

Binary thinking can also lead us to believe that anyone who demonstrates any level of resistance or disagreement with our position can and should be labeled a racist, naïve, prejudiced, "too woke," a lost cause, evil, or worse. Thinking that way is what makes it easy to conflate conflict with combat: the person we are speaking with is perceived as an enemy combatant. We fall victim to the predictable and pernicious psychological lure of sorting people into ingroups and outgroups. Thinking of people this way is counterproductive. It creates a bias that impacts our approach to the conversation, increasing the likelihood that the interaction will become adversarial. And if you believe someone is beyond your ability to reach and understand, then there's no reason to even try.

RECLAIM YOUR POWER

To feel confident going into a difficult conversation, we must believe that we can create positive change—that we can transform situations with our words and actions. That is the essence of the commonly misunderstood word *power*. When we talk about reclaiming your power, we are not discussing interpersonal influence or exerting positional authority. Reclaiming power, within this context, is denying someone else the ability to frame your mindset and internal narrative.

The term *locus of control* refers to how much people believe that they control the outcome of situations, rather than forces that are beyond their control. If you have a high locus of control as it relates to difficult conversations, you believe that your performance can and will have an impact on their outcomes. Unsurprisingly, your locus of control is closely related to your confidence.

You can have an impact. But, as cheesy as it sounds, you need to believe in yourself to make it happen.

Don't leave your success—or setbacks—in the hands of your conversation partner. When we blame the other person for how poorly a conversation went, without considering what we could have done differently to improve the situation ourselves, we give our power away. We reinforce the narrative that we are powerless in these interactions, and over time internalize the belief that these conversations are doomed to fail regardless of what we do.

Reclaiming your power is a vote of confidence in yourself. As habit and decision-making expert James Clear explains, "Every action you take is a vote for the type of person you wish to become. No single instance will transform your beliefs, but as the votes build up, so does the evidence of your identity."[4] Every time you lean courageously into one of these conversations, you are reminding yourself of what's possible, which makes the next conversation easier to have.

In my last book, which was all about overcoming your psychological and emotional barriers to performing well in difficult conversations, I talked about what I call the *Positive Cycle of Confidence*. One of the seemingly magical qualities of confidence is that it makes you more likely to act. It is a self-perpetuating phenomenon where confidence leads you to take more action, that action leads to positive results, and the results make you even more confident and more likely to take action in the future. Confidence both results in action and grows as a result of that action.[5]

There's no easy way around it. The best way to begin to reclaim your power in these conversations is by leaning in and having them. Every conversation is a practice opportunity.

When my team conducts negotiation trainings or conflict resolution coaching, one of the self-limiting beliefs that our clients often have to overcome is that they "aren't good at negotiation." I quickly correct them, saying, "You're not good at negotiation *yet*." In Carol Dweck's book *Mindset*, she identifies two different mindsets, the fixed mindset and the growth mindset.[6] Think of it as the difference between talent and skill. If you believe that your success is determined by talent, then what you do doesn't matter very much. You either have talent or you don't; if you don't have it now, you probably won't have it in the future. Skill, on the other hand, is something you can improve. A growth mindset recognizes that improvement is a possibility.

It is hard to do what you need to do when you do not believe you can. But with a simple change of mindset—and practice—you'll be able to improve your ability to perform in these crucial conversations. You may not be where you want to be right now, but you can get there.

BUT A LOT OF THESE CONVERSATIONS AREN'T EVEN ABOUT RACE, RIGHT?

Before I became a parent, I used to roll my eyes every time somebody would bring up their kids out of nowhere. We could be having a conversation about something completely unrelated to family—say, peanut butter—and then it was like they would go out of their way to throw the fact that they had kids in my face. I would think to myself, "Okay, okay, you have kids. I get it."

But I didn't get it. And now I'm that parent.

If I'm moving and considering neighborhoods, I have to think about my kids. If a friend wants to hang out, I have to think about my kids. If I have to travel for a speaking engagement, I have to think about my kids. When there is just a little bit of Cinnamon Toast Crunch left in the box, I have to think about my kids (because I don't want to share). Now that I have kids, I get it. But when I didn't have kids, not only did I not get it, but there was no way for me to get it. I had seen plenty of parents. Some of my best friends were parents. But I wasn't a parent.

It is extraordinarily difficult to *fully* appreciate how much one part of a person's identity can impact their life. When I told one of my White friends that I was going to put the story about being rejected on the playground into this book, they said, "I don't see the connection. I understand how that impacted your ability to have difficult conversations in general, but I don't get how it relates to this book about race." On the other hand, when I shared the same story with my BIPOC friends, they clearly saw the connection between race and rejection.

For many BIPOC, race has had such a profound impact on their lives that it's always top of mind. This is, in many ways, a survival mechanism: race has been a factor in so many situations in the past, often negatively, that they have developed a heightened awareness for it. It never crossed my White friend's mind that race might be at play because they grew up, and continue to live, in a predominantly White community. They've had the benefit of not having to consider the myriad ways race has affected their everyday lives.

This demonstrates a common challenge in conversations about race: *one of the parties involved might not even realize race is a factor.*

I once conducted a training where one of the managers, who was White, said, "Sometimes people come up to me with problems and they say that race played a role in the situation, but then when I hear the story, I don't think race played a role in it at all. I tell them that race doesn't have anything to do with the situation, but that never seems to work. Sometimes it makes it worse! What do we do in those situations?" The managers around him nodded in agreement.

I said, "Okay, I respect your perspective. I have a question for you. Does the person you're talking to think the situation is about race?"

"Yes."

"So whether or not *you personally* think it's about race, the mere fact that your conversation partner *does* think it's about race means that you're having a conversation about race. The conversation is going to be about race regardless of your perspective, because you're not the only person in the conversation who matters."

This isn't to say that, when a conversation is about race, it's *all* about race. Part of the challenge in these conversations is determining *how much* of a factor race played, if any. But as long as the person you're talking to feels as though race is involved, then the conversation is about race.[7]

When I spoke to a White friend about this, they said, "Kwame, it's not that I'm actively ignoring race as a factor or that I don't believe it's a legitimate factor. In fact, I wish I could consider it in order to be more inclusive. But sometimes it's not even in the realm of things I can think of as a possibility until someone else mentions it to me. How can I get myself to think of something that isn't in my conscious awareness?" A quick solution is to ask yourself, *How might race have played a role in this situation?*

I gave this piece of advice in a training and one of the participants brought up a great point. They said, "Yes, asking myself whether or not race played a role is helpful, but it doesn't address the fact that, as a White person, I still have blind spots. I might miss it even if I ask myself that question." This is an example of where a respectful question may be helpful. Simply saying, "I know I have some blind spots. What is something I am missing?" or "What else could be a factor?" during a conversation may be enough to get a colleague to share whether they see race as an issue.

When you're the person who perceives that race is a factor, it can be frustrating when the people around you struggle to see something that feels clear to you, and that has so significantly and painfully affected you in the past. But I hope this section can help you understand that what might seem obvious to you is not necessarily obvious to everyone. Rather than assuming that someone is discounting your experience out of indifference or malice and allowing that to keep you from engaging in these conversations, think about sharing your perspective.

I like to open with a question. For example, "We come from different backgrounds. What impact could that have on how we are seeing the situation?" This is designed to trigger empathy. The only way they can answer the question is by considering your perspective. It will also make them more open to hearing your perspective, because it will help them to realize that they may not fully understand your perspective. Rather than beginning the conversation from a place of contention, you can begin by working together to understand the situation, and each other, more completely.

YOU'RE NOT MAKING *ENOUGH* MISTAKES

I would be remiss if I did not acknowledge that there are legitimate risks when having these conversations:

- being accused of playing the race card
- being labeled a racist
- being ostracized
- being canceled
- losing a job
- losing a friend

Risk is a natural part of life, and if you want to be an effective leader and changemaker in your organization, you are going to have to talk about race. And although we cannot remove all risk, this book will provide you with both the skill set and mindset necessary to minimize these risks while maximizing effectiveness.

That doesn't mean you'll never make a mistake. The world is changing rapidly, and it can be overwhelming when it seems like new "rules" are coming up every day. But the biggest mistake you can make is avoiding these conversations. What does more damage in a relationship, trying your best and making a mistake or not trying at all?

Here's the thing: if you spend enough time with *anyone*, you will undoubtedly say or do something offensive, whether about race or something else. Offense is an unavoidable part of human interaction. In fact, if you're not making any mistakes, it's probably a sign that you're not spending enough time with people who are different from you. What matters is how you handle the moment of offense afterward: whether you are ashamed and shy away from further interactions, or reach out, make amends, and learn from it.

To be clear, I'm not advocating for you to go out, be reckless, and offend everybody. I'm saying that you need to not let fear of the mistakes that you will inevitably make stop you from having these conversations. Think back to Melanie and James. They took a risk. They shared their opinions. Did things turn out how they would've liked? No. Does it mean that they shouldn't have said anything? No.

Maya Angelou said, "Do the best you can until you know better. Then when you know better, do better." I would take it a step further: when you know better, do better, *and forgive yourself when you fall short*. If you are a person who is willing to read a book titled *How to Have Difficult Conversations About Race*, you're likely already approaching these conversations with a baseline level of respect for the other person. That alone will lead you to make fewer mistakes. Beating yourself up over a misstep is counterproductive. Learn what you can do better next time and move on.

Self-forgiveness and self-compassion are the unsung heroes behind self-confidence. On the front end, they reduce the fear and anxiety that can paralyze you, because they quiet your inner critic. They also give you the resilience you need to come back stronger if you do fail.

Further, I'm willing to bet that if you were to list all of the mistakes you can remember making in difficult conversations about race and compare it to the total number of conversations you've ever had on the topic, your failure rate would be much lower than you think. We tend to magnify past mistakes due to *negativity bias*, "our tendency not only to register negative stimuli more readily but also to dwell on these events."[8] In other words, we remember the bad more than the good.

Still feeling nervous? Consider providing a disclaimer, which can minimize the negative impact of the mistakes that you make. Begin by telling your conversation partner that this is a tough subject, you do not know all the answers, and you are still learning. Express how you are hoping that each of you can learn from each other. Having openly expressed your fears, and assured the person you're speaking with of your positive intent, you can start your conversation with greater confidence. A disclaimer also allows you to take control of the situation so that even if something bad does occur, it does less damage. Though you may still say something offensive, your conversation partner is less likely to be offended.

As a young lawyer entering the Supreme Court mentoring program, I was paired with Mark Decker, a White lawyer in his sixties. Mark, who described himself as a "dyed-in-the-wool conservative," was a no nonsense, straight-to-the-point kind of guy. In our first meeting, he said, "I'm an old dog, and you're a young pup. My job is to teach you how to be a better lawyer and I take that responsibility very seriously, but before we start, there's something I need to tell you.

"I consider myself to be a good person, but there have been times in my life that people have called me a racist and I don't know why. I don't know what I did or said to earn that title and I feel horrible about it. So I want you to know, there will probably be times where I say or do something offensive. I apologize in advance for that. It's not my intent. All that I ask is that you let me know those times so I can get better."

Now, you don't need to go that deep with your disclaimer. You can say something like, "We have different backgrounds and different life experiences. It's likely that, as we work together, there will be some miscommunications, and it's possible that I will say or do something offensive. I care about making sure we have a great working relationship, and I want you to feel comfortable letting me know when that occurs so I can be a better colleague to you."

This sort of simple disclaimer gives you a little bit of grace for those inevitable mistakes. Did Mark make mistakes? Absolutely. But they led to some fantastic conversations. He's had an incredibly positive impact on my career and we're still friends to this day. In turn, he was able to learn and get better. I guess you *can* teach an old dog new tricks.

OVERCOMING YOUR FEARS

Kim used to be a proud ally for racial equity until a casual conversation with a diverse group of friends shook her confidence, both at work and outside of it. While discussing Amy Cooper, the White woman who called the NYPD on a Black man who'd asked her to leash her dog per Central Park rules, Kim agreed that it was appropriate for Amy Cooper to be publicly shamed and possibly lose her job, but added she thought the authorities should *not* press charges. In response, one of her friends said, "Amy Cooper tried to weaponize the police to threaten the life of a Black man just because he asked her to follow the law," argued that Amy Cooper deserved jail time, and told Kim to "check her privilege." The two friends haven't spoken since.

Kim was left terrified at the prospect of having difficult conversations about race. At work, she was afraid that her relationships within the company, and possibly her employment, would be at risk if somebody deemed what she said to be inappropriate. Any time a conversation about race came up, she would either listen silently or excuse herself entirely, unwilling to risk engaging.

When I work with clients trying to overcome past fears or psychological barriers, I gain inspiration from cognitive behavioral therapy (CBT) techniques. *To be clear, I am not a licensed therapist, nor do I practice therapy.* And I am not suggesting that everyone who has had a negative experience regarding race relations needs therapy (although if you have had past traumatic experiences that affect your everyday life, please do discuss this with a licensed therapist). However, I believe we can all benefit from incorporating CBT principles in overcoming our everyday challenges.

Cognitive behavioral therapy attempts to modify thought patterns to change behaviors and moods. The theory behind CBT is that negative feelings or actions come from distorted beliefs.[9] If you can change your beliefs, you can change your behaviors. And if you can change your behaviors, you can improve your outcomes.

For example, one type of CBT is exposure therapy, in which a person is safely and gradually exposed to the thing that causes distress. When people are afraid, "they often avoid anything that reminds them of [their fear]. This avoidance provides temporary relief but ultimately maintains the fear and pattern of avoidance."[10] You can use your own version of exposure therapy to slowly increase your confidence during difficult conversations. Find opportunities to practice in low-stakes scenarios. Discuss a thorny race-related topic with your partner or a close friend and then ask them for feedback so you can improve.

In Kim's case, our team worked with her to get more comfortable and confident in these conversations because she realized that, given her position in the company, she couldn't avoid them forever. And, more importantly, she wanted to be an ally and knew these conversations were a necessary part of that.

First, we helped her identify the negative thought patterns caused by her underlying fear. When Kim thought about how a difficult conversation would go, she would imagine the following:

1. She says anything on the topic.
2. Someone accuses her of being racist, insensitive, or privileged.
3. She tries to apologize and explain herself to no avail.
4. She loses friends and social status within her company.

Next, we took steps to replace this problematic thought pattern with something that was more empowering and would ultimately enable her to have these vital conversations. To challenge her fear-based assumptions, Kim and I role-played conversations and found other opportunities for her to have low-stakes conversations on race with friends and family. This accumulation of small wins helped build her confidence.

Then, I suggested Kim host listening sessions with her employees on race-related issues that people were facing in the company. All she had to do was follow a few brief rules:

1. Acknowledge the emotions that she saw in the people she was talking to.
2. Ask open-ended questions for them to share their truths.
3. Listen more than she speaks.

These provided Kim with several opportunities to experience these conversations and leave them unscathed. The less Kim spoke, the less likely it was that she could make a mistake. It also gave her a chance to listen and digest what was being said without anyone expecting her to respond. This process helped her feel more confident ahead of the high-stakes conversations she wanted to have about race with company leaders.

Identifying problematic thought patterns and replacing them with those that are more positive, helpful, and empowering is the key to creating a confident mindset. Your solution may not be the same as Kim's, because your fears are different, but her story at least offers a glimpse into how the process works.

The crucial inner work in this chapter is the first step to having effective conversations. The next step is to gain a better understanding of the psychological roadblocks—both yours and your conversation partner's—that can derail these conversations, and how to avoid or resolve them when they occur.

DISCUSSION QUESTIONS

- What makes difficult conversations about race challenging for you?
- Since labeling emotions is the first step to managing them, what are three emotions that you feel when you are confronted with conversations about race?
- What problematic or disempowering thought patterns do you have?
- What experiences have you had, or what events have you observed, that led you to feel this way?
- What more positive and productive thought processes can you utilize to help you move past your fears?

CHAPTER
THREE

COMMON PSYCHOLOGICAL BARRIERS

A s a negotiation consultant, I've had the opportunity to advise businesses on deals worth hundreds of millions of dollars. Needless to say, there's a lot on the line and tensions run high. Yet the level of emotion I've seen in these large business deals pales in comparison to what I've seen in these difficult workplace conversations about race. Why? Because discussions about race draw on strongly held beliefs about identity (who we are) and morality (what it means to be a good or bad person). In other words, conversations about race inevitably involve how we see ourselves and how we want others to see us. Therefore, when people disagree with our ideas or perspectives on the topic of race, the rejection feels personal.

When discussing highly emotional subjects like race, we can be quick to disregard someone else's emotions or beliefs because we do not feel they have the right to feel the way they do. We hear someone talking about feeling hurt by a microaggression, then mentally roll our eyes and call them oversensitive, or disregard someone's trepidation about specific inclusion strategies at work because we look at them and only see a life of privilege. The problem is that emotions don't play by our rules. If you dismiss someone's emotions, for any reason, all you do is amplify those feelings and create an even larger barrier for yourself to overcome during the conversation. Denying the way someone feels is a recipe for disaster, no matter what you are trying to accomplish.

We all share a beautifully complex set of psychological tendencies and emotional responses that have a significant impact on how we engage in these crucial conversations. And if we don't handle them appropriately, these responses will likely poison our interactions with one another, and prevent us from reaching our goals.

According to astrophysicist Neil DeGrasse Tyson, "In science, when human behavior enters the equation, things go nonlinear. That's why Physics is easy and Sociology is hard." One of the biggest challenges we have in difficult conversations is appreciating the complex ways that psychology affects perception and communication—especially during conversations about race. In difficult conversations, our psychological responses are broadly predictable, because, as human beings, we're all more or less using the same operating system. However, the way your operating system functions depends on the situation, your individual perspective, and your lived experience. Digging into this psychology can help you more clearly understand the challenges we face so we can get clear about the solutions. It's almost impossible to overcome a barrier if you can't see the barrier.

Before we begin, it's important to remember, as you read more about our psychological tendencies, that they don't make us bad; they make us human. When you're able to anticipate these psychological and emotional challenges, *both in yourself and others*, it will reduce the harm they inflict on you and on your conversations about race.

In this chapter I discuss some of the most common psychological barriers that poison our conversations and our ability to think clearly and effectively during them, and provide antidotes.

IMPLICIT BIAS

We most often hear the term *bias* when referring to prejudice against people arising from things like race, gender, sexual orientation, or disability. But more broadly, a bias is just a preference toward something or a prejudice against something.

We all exhibit bias, in some form, in all aspects of our lives. In fact, I'd go as far as to say that bias is our natural state of mind. Every day, in the course of normal living, we have to make an endless number of decisions. If we had to start from scratch every time we were faced with a choice—Which toothpaste brand should I use? What cereal should I eat?—we wouldn't have enough cognitive energy to make it past breakfast. To make things easier on us, the brain organizes the incredible amount of information it receives into categories, which we then rarely revisit: *good toothpaste* vs. *bad toothpaste, breakfast cereal I like* vs. *breakfast cereal I don't like.*[1] This allows us to go through most of our day without too much cognitive effort.

For example, which shoe do you put on first, your left or your right? You might not know the answer offhand, but I'd bet you do it the same way most days. Why? Who knows. Maybe you put your left shoe on first because you're left-handed. Maybe you do it because your *father* is left-handed, and so that's how he taught you to put them on. Regardless of the reason, you have a particular preference. And relying on this preference, rather than deciding which shoe to start with every time, makes getting dressed in the morning much faster and easier.

Bias doesn't only affect our decision making. It also impacts how we perceive objective reality. In one study, researchers performed an experiment where they had participants taste wine while in an MRI scanner in order to record their brain activity. The researchers showed participants the price of a wine, allowed them to sample that wine, then asked them to rate it based on how much they enjoyed it—all while monitoring their brain activity. The researchers then repeated the steps with a differently priced wine.

What the participants didn't know was that they were given the *same* wine both times. The only difference between the wines was how much the participants were told they cost. Yet the subjects reported that the more expensive wine tasted better than the cheaper one. What's even more fascinating is that the participants' brain activity was greater when they tasted the wine with the higher price point—indicating that they *genuinely perceived a difference in taste because of their beliefs about the wine.*[2]

Have you ever heard the saying that perception is reality? Here, we mean that in the literal sense. Just as the participants in the wine study were convinced that the "expensive" wine tasted better, we all *genuinely believe* in the objectivity of our position—even when our position is anything but.

The most dangerous bias you can have is that you are unbiased—because the most insidious biases are the ones we don't realize we have.

Some biases we are aware of. For example, we prefer tea over coffee; we like Ohio State, we don't like Michigan. Others—like which shoe we put on first, or what kinds of people are more industrious or intelligent—are what scientists would call an *implicit bias.*

Implicit biases are preferences or prejudices that result from unconscious associations and feelings. Because these biases are unconscious, they don't necessarily line up with our explicitly stated beliefs. If I asked you if it's better to put on your left shoe first, you'd probably be confused and say no—and then struggle to explain why you nonetheless choose to put your left shoe on first 92 percent of the time.[*]

Many implicit biases are harmless. But others have real-world consequences that go beyond preferring an expensive Petrus Bordeaux Blend when a five-dollar bottle of rosé would get the job done.

I was a psychology tutor in undergrad, and one of the students I tutored was from South Korea. We lived close to each other, so we would walk back to the dorms together after our sessions and chat. One time, we ran into one of my friends and, in the course of our conversation, I mentioned that we were just leaving a tutoring session. My friend asked me, "Oh, what's he

---

[*] If you want to dig further into implicit bias, I suggest reading Daniel Kahneman's *Thinking, Fast and Slow.* It's more than six hundred pages and still does not fully cover all the science this brief section references.

tutoring you in?" My friend didn't know the student from South Korea at all, but he assumed that the Asian student was tutoring the Black student, not the other way around.

When someone with this kind of implicit bias is in a position of power, that can have significant consequences. In March 2021, Sandra Sellers, a professor of negotiation and mediation at Georgetown Law, was fired after being recorded on a Zoom call with a colleague saying, "I end up having this angst every semester that a lot of my lower ones are Blacks . . . Happens almost every semester. And it's like, 'Oh, come on.' It's some really good ones, but there are also usually some that are just plain at the bottom, it drives me crazy."[3]

I'm a professor of negotiation and mediation at the law school and MBA level. I know that in these courses, you don't base grades only on the outcome—you also base them on the process. There's an art to it. And, like art, it can be extremely subjective. Sometimes there are cultural or stylistic differences in the ways students from different racial backgrounds articulate themselves, and it's possible that, because of implicit bias, Sellers treated those differences as actually being wrong or less effective rather than different. It's easy for professors to conflate *their* way with the *right* way. Did her Black students underperform? Or did she simply perceive them as underperforming, the way the wine-study participants perceived the "expensive" wine to be higher in quality?

The implicit biases of others can also directly affect performance. In one research study, teachers were told that certain students, labeled "bloomers," scored higher on an IQ test than their peers and that, according to the test results, the teachers could expect them to do better than their classmates throughout the year. Then the researchers told the teachers the names of the students. What the teachers didn't know was that these students were chosen at random. *They weren't really high achievers.* Nonetheless, at the end of the school year, those labeled as "bloomers" performed better than their peers on the subsequent IQ tests. The bloomer label created a self-fulling prophecy where the teachers unwittingly provided more time, resources, and attention to the children they believed were more likely to succeed, which in turn led to their greater success.[4]

In conversations about race, it's important to remember that both we and our conversation partner are unavoidably operating from our own implicit biases. These biases affect what we see as a problem, and what we consider viable solutions. They affect how we see each other, and how we hear what the other person is saying.

Antidote for Implicit Bias: Self-Awareness and Introspection

Because we can't change our implicit biases (and the decisions and behaviors they lead to) unless we realize we have them, the first step to overcoming our biases is recognizing them. To do so, you have to be willing to slow down and question your assumptions. A quick reality check can help. When you are making a decision or trying to come to a conclusion, just ask yourself these two questions:

- What assumption am I making?
- How do I know this to be true?

That will help you to think through the situation more objectively, and as a result, will increase the likelihood that you are basing your decision on reason and data rather than feelings and bias.

Here's an example. Let's say you're a manager, and you have an implicit bias that leads you to assume that *all* Hispanic or Latinx people you encounter speak English as a second language and thus don't communicate at a level that's comparable to yours. You're hiring for a position in your department that requires strong communication skills, and immediately start to move a candidate with a Hispanic last name into the "no" pile. Before you do, slow down and do a quick bias check, based on the preceding questions.

What assumption am I making? Because this person is Latinx, they don't have a firm grasp on the English language.

How do I know this to be true? Well, I don't. I don't know whether English is their second language. And, even if I did, it doesn't mean their language skills are less competent than mine.

We need to develop the habit of slowing down and examining our thought processes to make sure bias isn't creeping in. Assume that bias is having an impact on how you think and act, because it probably is. Then work to minimize that impact with a bias check.

ATTRIBUTION BIAS

Another common bias we encounter in conversations about race is *attribution bias*—the tendency to attribute someone's behavior to internal causes and static qualities rather than the person's current situation or circumstances.[5] Attribution bias comes into play whenever we try to determine why someone does what they do, says what they say, or believes what they believe. For example, say you use a friend's bathroom and discover the toilet paper roll is hung so that the paper emerges from the bottom—when everyone knows the better way to hang a toilet paper roll is so that the end hangs over the top. Attribution bias may lead you to conclude that your friend has put the roll on improperly because they are uncivilized—but it might just mean they were in a hurry that morning and put it on backwards by accident this one time.

One of the most prevalent mistakes that results from this bias is known as *fundamental attribution error*. This is where we overestimate personality-based explanations for *others'* negative behaviors, underestimating potential situational explanations, while simultaneously interpreting our own negative actions in the opposite way.[6]

Here's a classic example. Let's say you're running late for work and you're driving twenty miles per hour over the speed limit. Why are you speeding? Because you're late.

Now, let's say that you're driving the speed limit and someone else drives past you going twenty miles per hour over the speed limit. Why are they speeding? Because they're reckless and irresponsible.

As humans, we are always looking for reasons for why people do what they do, even if we do so only subconsciously. Oftentimes, if we're not exactly sure why someone did what they did, we lean toward a negative interpretation of their behavior. After all, assuming malicious intent kept us safe in the early days of humanity. If your distant ancestors were in the wilderness by themselves, heard something behind them, and assumed the source of the sound wasn't a threat when it actually was, it might have been their last mistake. The ones who assumed situations like these *were* something dangerous and operating with intent to cause harm were also more likely to stay alive—and they passed that bias on to you.

In my TEDx talk, "Finding Confidence in Conflict," I mentioned that society has evolved faster than our brains. Because of this, we are fighting modern-day battles with often maladaptive prehistoric tools.[7] Our tendency to assume malicious intent damages our ability to communicate and connect.

A few years ago, a community organization in Canada reached out to me to conduct a mediation between a local police department and a Black family. The family believed they had received unfair, racially motivated treatment from a police officer and wanted to ensure that the same thing didn't happen to other BIPOC in the community.

During the mediation I heard both sides of the story, reviewed the policies and procedures that were at play, and realized that, from a legal perspective, everything was done by the book. However, even if something was done legally, it doesn't mean that it was done equitably. And I needed to help the leaders in the police department understand why, although policies and procedures were followed appropriately, it didn't make a difference to the family and the community in terms of perception and emotion.

ME: I agree that, based on what the family told me and what you're telling me, your officer followed the rules. But here's the thing: it really doesn't matter whether or not you did everything right.

THEM: (*shocked and confused*): What do you mean?

ME: Perception is reality. If you do everything right but people don't believe that you did everything right, then, in their eyes, you *didn't* do it right. They don't *feel* like they were treated fairly and that's why we're here.

THEM: I see what you're saying, Kwame. The thing is, there is an art to policing. It's kind of like customer service. Some officers just aren't good at that part.

ME: That makes a lot of sense and I agree. I think that's what happened here. But let's look at two different scenarios. Let's say a White police officer does everything the right way but he's a jerk to a White person during a traffic stop—what does that White person think?

THEM: Well, they probably think that guy is a jerk.

ME: Exactly. Now imagine the exact same scenario where the White police officer does everything by the book but he's a jerk to a Black person at a traffic stop. What does that person think?

THEM ("AHA!" MOMENT): They think it's because of racism.

ME: Exactly. Look at the news over the last year. Black people have been primed to be wary of the police, and for good reason. Race may not have factored into how you and your team handled this interaction, but you're being viewed in that light.

In other words, because of attribution bias, the family that made the complaint interpreted what they perceived as the officer's cold and inflexible application of the rules as due to racism rather than the officer being procedurally handcuffed and trying his best to do his job.

Thankfully, the police and the family were able to reconcile their differences and even discuss policy changes that would make it less likely that other people would have the same experience. They used the conflict as an opportunity to create positive change in their community. But you can see how the underlying psychology at play tainted the larger conversation and made it more difficult to find a productive solution.

In some cases, fundamental attribution error can serve as a negative self-fulfilling prophecy. For example, let's say that you're having a meeting with someone and you believe that they will not look favorably upon you or your work because of your race. As a result, you lose faith in your ability to succeed in the interaction. You don't prepare as much and lack enthusiasm and confidence during the meeting. This behavior actually leads them to view you unfavorably, confirming your original faulty hypothesis.

Antidote for Attribution Bias, Part 1: Assume Positive Intent

I'm going to share an outside-the-box, and possibly controversial, mental trick I use to improve my performance in difficult conversations: *helpful fiction*. A helpful fiction is an intentionally manufactured positive story that's designed to overcome problematic negative biases.

Thanks to attribution bias, we tend to assume the worst of others. For me, the key to overcoming this isn't just awareness that the bias exists; it's replacing that bias with a helpful—and plausible—fiction. In difficult conversations, instead of assuming negative intent, I assume positive intent. And I do this by giving people the benefit of the doubt.

One of the most radical parts of my previous book, *Finding Confidence in Conflict*, was called "the benefit of the benefit of the doubt." Giving someone the benefit of the doubt means believing that they are trying the best they can in the situation, given their beliefs, skills, emotions, and current perception. With this mindset, you are less likely to see their behavior as threatening, which makes it less likely for negative attributional biases to creep in.

Giving others the benefit of the doubt in difficult conversations is also a smart strategic choice. While it might seem naïve or foolish, it actually puts you in a better position for success. People often perform to your level of expectation. When you assume the worst, they perform poorly. If you assume the best, they perform better. It also makes it easier for you to focus on the conversation at hand because you're not burdened with the emotions associated with assuming the worst.

For example, in my mediations, I grant participants the benefit of the doubt by giving them an excuse. Let's say one party is hostile and aggressive. As a mediator, I need to remain impartial, and I know that if I respond too aggressively, it might give them the opportunity to question my impartiality. The way that I assume positive intent here is by inventing scenarios that explain why they are behaving the way they are. Maybe their dog died, or maybe they have a sick parent. Likely there's a lot of pressure on them, and they may be in a new situation where they don't know how to act. This prevents me from taking their reactions personally and allows me to stay focused.

I know some of you are saying, "Come on, Kwame. The person I'm dealing with has done some pretty awful things." I believe you. I've certainly been in situations like that in my career, too. In those cases, I still assume the other person is trying their best—it's just that at the moment, their best isn't very good. This helps me keep my cool and conduct myself in a respectable fashion even when the person I'm speaking to is behaving badly, which protects my reputation. Because I am a Black lawyer, I believe that it is easier for people to attach negative stigma to my behavior, even when I'm justified in my actions, so I choose to always carry myself in these conversations as if somebody that I care about and respect is watching.

Simply acknowledging another person's words and actions while withholding judgment will help protect you from rushing to conclusions about their intent and character, which will also protect you from basing your response on flawed information. The reality is, we never know for sure what's in someone's heart. Therefore, why not *choose* to interpret their actions and intent in a way that is beneficial to your own performance?

Giving others the benefit of the doubt has another important benefit. Some people intentionally use underhanded, manipulative tactics designed to create pressure, anxiety, and emotional distress in order to "win" a difficult conversation. Believing the best of others shields you from the psychological effects of those tactics. Also, some people are confrontational by nature. They love a good fight. When you insist on assuming their intent is positive, you show that you're not going to play that game, and they tend to become more compliant and collaborative. They realize those tricks won't work on you, and they respect your resilience.

The benefit of the doubt is a gift you give yourself. It allows you to avoid taking things personally, which makes it easier for you to manage your emotions and perform at a higher level, and improves your odds of succeeding in the conversation.

Antidote for Attribution Bias, Part 2: Stop Manifesting Failure, Believe You Can Succeed

Because attribution bias leads us to believe others' behavior has to do with something internal and static (e.g., they're inconsiderate or racist), we often tell ourselves an *unhelpful* fiction about our ability to connect and communicate with them: *we choose to believe that it's just not possible.*

Remember how attribution error can be a self-fulfilling prophecy? Many times we struggle in difficult conversations and fail to meet our goals simply because we don't believe we can succeed at them. You can overcome this by telling yourself you can. When you start out, this might remain a helpful fiction. But your ability to connect and persuade is more powerful than you realize. You just need to have the confidence, resilience, and persistence to succeed.

Confidence is crucial to success. Steph Curry, the best three-point shooter in the NBA, says, "Every time I rise up, I have confidence that I'm going to make it." Does this mean he's going to make every shot? No. But *he believes he can* when he's shooting. Likewise, when I go into difficult conversations, I believe I can connect with and persuade the other person, whoever they may be.

Daryl Davis is a Black man with a fascinating hobby: he befriends members of the Ku Klux Klan (KKK). "The oldest and most infamous of American hate groups" and "America's longest standing terrorist organization," the KKK has, over the course of American history, murdered and assaulted thousands. Their targets have included Jewish, Catholic, and LGBTQ+ people, as well as immigrants, but they have primarily focused on Black Americans.[8] Despite the KKK's legacy of hatred and violence, Davis says he's been able to convince two hundred Klansmen to renounce their membership and change their lives.[9]

How can Davis, a Black man, connect with KKK members on such a deep level that they can change their foundational beliefs? It comes down to courage, persistence, respect—and, of course, the radical belief that it's possible to do so.

Racism never made sense to Davis, because, as he wondered, "How can you hate me if you don't know me?" Seeking an answer to that question, he decided to go straight to the source. He had his secretary arrange a meeting with Roger Kelly, then the KKK's national leader, while omitting the fact that Davis was Black.

Kelly arrived to their scheduled meeting with an armed bodyguard, and as soon as they saw Davis, both men froze. Davis stood up, showed that he wasn't armed, and extended his hand to greet Kelly. Kelly and the bodyguard each shook his hand and a very tense conversation ensued.

According to Davis, although the conversation was productive, Kelly "let me know that I was not his equal. I was inferior; he was superior. And this was justified and determined by the color of my skin."

But Davis was there on a specific mission, and he wasn't going to allow the offense to distract or deter him. "I wasn't there to fight him; I was there to learn from him: where does this ideology come from? Because once you learn where it comes from, you can then try to figure out how to address it and see where it's going."

What Davis learned was that "ignorance breeds fear. We fear those things we do not understand. If we do not keep that fear in check, that fear, in turn, will breed hatred because we hate those things that frighten us." Davis decided that he would continue to build his relationship with Kelly so that Kelly could become familiar with the people he feared and hated.

Over the next few years, he would frequently invite Kelly to his home to continue the conversation. At times, he would also invite Black friends, Jewish friends, and open-minded White friends so that Kelly could interact with more people from diverse backgrounds. The relationship deepened over the years. Kelly invited Davis to his house in return and even to Klan rallies. Davis went to the rallies not because he agreed with what was being said there, but in order to observe and learn. After he spent a couple of years creating a meaningful relationship with Kelly and learning about his beliefs and opinions, even though they were radically different from his own, Davis was able to persuade Kelly, the national leader of the KKK, to leave the Klan.

Obviously, this is a very extreme example, but I wanted to include it to demonstrate how your ability to connect and persuade is far more powerful than you might think. If Davis can get the head of the Klan to leave the organization, you can talk to your coworker about why you believe your organization needs to change in ways that make the workplace more diverse, inclusive, and equitable.

CONFIRMATION BIAS

Confirmation bias is the tendency to search for, interpret, favor, and recall information in a way that confirms or supports one's prior beliefs or values. We tend to unconsciously select information that supports our views while ignoring nonsupportive or contradicting information.[10] Rather than looking at the evidence, thinking rationally about it, and then arriving at a conclusion, we tend to start with our preferred conclusion and then look for evidence to support it. Essentially, we have conclusions running around in search of evidence.

You can see how confirmation bias works by imagining the difference in the results you'd get from searching *what shape is the earth* versus *flat earth truth* versus *round earth hoax*. We do a good job of convincing ourselves that we're looking for the truth, when in fact we're really just searching for *our truth*. With the power of almighty Google, all beliefs are possible.

The reason confirmation bias is so dangerous is that we *genuinely believe we have come to our conclusions after a rational evaluation of the evidence*, despite those conclusions sometimes seeming nonsensical to others.

I love watching mixed martial arts videos on YouTube, which is where I learned about "energy shield masters," who claim to physically disable opponents using an invisible "energy." In videos, the masters dramatically flail their arms while multiple acolytes try to attack them, and the "energy" knocks the students over before they get close enough to land a punch. Some of the energy masters boast they've had hundreds of fights and never lost. But every so often a video of an energy master taking on a *real* martial artist surfaces, and the result is worth all the time I've wasted entertaining myself. Without going into graphic detail, let's say only that the real fighter, who is (shockingly) unfazed by the alleged energy, easily wins the fight.

Why in the world would an "energy master" go toe to toe with a real martial artist? Confirmation bias. In this case, they have chosen to believe they have special abilities despite what I have to assume has been overwhelming evidence to the contrary, because, on a deep level, *they want it to be true.* (Listen, I loved *Dragon Ball Z* at a young age, too, but, after seeing the evidence, I reluctantly had to come to the conclusion that I didn't have magical powers.) But the most impressive example of the power of confirmation bias is seen in the response of the energy masters after the fight. They don't come to terms with the reality of the situation; they offer excuses. They'll blame their loss on an illness, for example, rather than the concussive force of unimpeded punches.[11]

In many cases, when someone has a belief they hold dear, it's not merely something that they believe. *The belief is part of who they are.* To them, denying that belief is tantamount to denying their personhood. The prospect of adjusting their beliefs creates an existential crisis, which they resolve by reinterpreting reality to ensure that belief—and thus their identity—remains intact.

Have you ever had a conversation where it seemed as though the other person was impervious to the facts? Confirmation bias might have been the culprit. It's why trying to persuade somebody by sheer force of data, evidence, and statistics is often not enough. The other person will always find a way to deny or reinterpret the data to support their existing belief.

Confirmation bias can come from a good place, but it almost never leads to a good outcome. For example, one of my friends confided in me that, "Whenever a BIPOC colleague talks about a microaggression they experienced, I noticed that I have this tendency to just say, 'Oh, I'm sure the other person didn't mean it that way.' I've seen a lot of my White colleagues do the same thing. It's like we're trying to justify what happened and explain it away by either saying that what happened was unintentional or minimizing it by saying it wasn't that bad. Why do we do that?"

One reason I think good people make this mistake is that they don't like racism and don't want it to exist. Because of that, and because of confirmation bias, they are going to be drawn to explanations for behavior in which racism doesn't come into play. And if they can convince their BIPOC friend that what happened wasn't racist, they think it will make their friend feel better. Also, it's likely that, especially at work, they have a relationship with both parties: the perpetrator and the recipient. So not only do they want the person who was the victim to feel better, they also don't want to interpret the situation in a way that makes their colleague, who is also a friend, seem racist.

The trouble is, in trying to find a way to protect both of them, it minimizes the experience of the person who was hurt. *The heartbeat of racism is denial.*[12] Despite my friend's positive intentions, by filtering the interaction through his preferred conclusion that racism wasn't at play, he was denying the impact of racism in a way that was hurtful. This is less helpful encouragement than it is racial gaslighting. (Gaslighting is "the act of undermining another person's reality by denying facts, the environment around them, or their feelings."[13]) And you can't solve a problem if you can't, or won't, see the problem.

The confidence confirmation bias gives us in our own beliefs can also lead us to something that I call *reflexive rejection.* Likely there have been times when you were having a conversation and the other person began to disagree with you before you even finished your thought. This can be frustrating. How can they disagree if they don't even know what you're going to say?

Here, bias is preventing the other person from meaningfully considering what you have to say. It's not even that they disagree with you, per se (or that they would, if they stopped and listened); it's just that their defenses are up. They're protecting themselves from having to wrestle with the potential legitimacy of your claim.

Reflexive rejection comes up frequently in conversations about race because the more emotional the conversation and the more deeply held the beliefs that conversation is challenging, the more threatening it feels and the more defensive we tend to get.

Antidote for Confirmation Bias and Reflexive Rejection: Perspective Expansion

When you read the previous section, examples of confirmation bias and reflexive rejection in other people probably came to mind. But both phenomena live in all of us. And the key to combating them, in ourselves and others, is *perspective expansion*.

In the folktale "The Blind Men and the Elephant," six blind men are asked to describe an elephant based on touch. Each gives a completely different description. One man describes the elephant as like a fan; another describes it as like a dangerous, deadly spear.[14] An argument ensues.

Which man was correct? None of them—and yet all of them. Each man correctly described what they felt: the man who described the elephant as a fan was touching the elephant's ear; the man who described the elephant as a spear was touching the tusk. But each man's perspective was limited.

Usually, in conversations on complex issues like race, when there is a vehement disagreement, a major part of the challenge comes down to issues of perception. What I find in a lot of my conversations is that it's very rare that someone is 100 percent wrong in their perspective. Rather, they are only seeing one small part of the elephant, and are overconfident in their extrapolation of what they know about the whole.

One time I looked in the backyard and saw my son Kai standing on a chair, reaching up into the sky. He was two at the time. I asked him what he was doing and he said, "I'm trying to touch the moon, Daddy." It was a cute but fruitless endeavor. Why did he believe he could touch the moon? His lack of knowledge—about perspective and size and space—made it seem feasible. Kai was a victim of the Dunning-Kruger effect, a cognitive bias in which we wrongly overestimate our knowledge or ability in a particular area. It's why people with the least amount of information so often seem to be the most confident in their positions. They simply don't know enough to understand how little they know. Not surprisingly, the Dunning-Kruger effect is likely to play a role in how people understand, and misunderstand, the complex issues around race, which makes confirmation bias more difficult to overcome.

To fight confirmation bias and avoid reflexive rejection, in yourself and others, focus on expanding perspective. When I realize that my conversation partner and I see things very differently, rather than starting the interaction by directly challenging others' beliefs, I start by trying to help them to see more of the proverbial elephant by asking questions that let them realize there is more to be seen. If you approach it this way, the person is more likely to be willing to go on the journey with you.

Instead of telling one of the blind men, "You're wrong, an elephant isn't like a fan," I say, "I understand how you could believe that considering your lived experience and your perspective. What do you think about the elephant's leg?"

"Leg?" he asks. "I didn't even know it had a leg."

"Oh, okay. That makes sense. Come with me, let's walk there together."

Remember, it's not just confirmation bias in others you'll need to watch out for in difficult conversations about race; confirmation bias is something we all struggle with. If you're in a conversation and realize that you've come to a conclusion before you've heard the other person's explanation, or that you're constructing your counterpoint instead of listening to what they're saying, confirmation bias is likely playing a role. Patience is critical. Take advantage of the opportunity to learn.

After you listen to their point and consider what they have to say, you may still come to the conclusion that they're wrong. That's perfectly fine. But you may be surprised to find that you agree on much more than you originally thought. As you try to expand others' perspectives, don't be afraid to open yourself up to new perspectives as well.

CURSE OF KNOWLEDGE

The *curse of knowledge* is a cognitive bias where you assume that your conversational partner has the foundational understanding necessary to make sense of what you're saying, because that understanding feels so obvious to you.[15] When we learn something, we often forget how it feels to not know it. As a result, we tend to communicate with other people as if they are starting from the same level of knowledge about a topic that we are—and then get angry when they don't understand what we're saying.

In many ways, the more depth of knowledge you have about something, the harder it can be to break it down for people who are newer to the topic. If someone doesn't know *anything* about structural racism, for example, and you're trying to convince them that taking personal responsibility for one's academic success isn't, by itself, a sufficient antidote to racial equity issues in America's school system, then leading with dense statistics and data won't work—in fact it can be overwhelming. You need to start conversations by establishing a baseline of mutual understanding—in this case, leveling on what a child needs to be successful and how they come to access those things may be a more realistic place to start. Otherwise, it's like a sixteen-year-old getting mad at a six-year-old for their inability to understand calculus.

Antidote for Curse of Knowledge: The Blessing of Baby Steps

We've all heard the saying "Take baby steps." The idea that we need to move incrementally toward our goals applies in difficult conversations as well. We often start a conversation in a very different place from that of the person we're talking to. We need to figure out where they are in their understanding, and start from there, using baby steps to catch them up until you're both working with the same set of foundational facts.

Let's use that example of structural racism in schools. If you recognize at the beginning of the conversation that there's a disconnect between your understanding of the term and the other person's, you could say something like, "Let's take a step back. What do you know about how schools are funded in America?" If they say they have no clue, then you know that's where the conversation needs to start—a *completely* different place from where you might have expected. How can you discuss solutions if the other person doesn't yet understand the problem? Instead of talking about the impact of different levels of access to school resources on the success of individual students, you'd begin the conversation talking about the discrepancy in funding between schools that are majority white and schools that are majority BIPOC.

Keep in mind, that discussion of funding discrepancy might be an entire conversation by itself. Remember the idea of micro-negotiations? Think of micro-negotiations as their own kinds of baby steps, each one bringing you closer to your ultimate goal.

JUST WORLD FALLACY

Another key psychological barrier that frequently comes up in conversations about race is the *just world fallacy*: the belief that the world is a fair and equitable place.

There's security in believing the just world fallacy. You can take solace in the idea that the input of hard work consistently nets the output of success and that the input of good decisions consistently nets the output of safety.

The existence of racism is incompatible with this belief that the world is fair. If racism exists, then people are getting bad outcomes regardless of their inputs. The prospect of this can be frightening for some people, because realizing that the world isn't fair for others means that there are situations in which the world won't be fair to them—and that their personal success might not be due solely to hard work. That's a hard reality to accept.

At the American Negotiation Institute, we regularly survey the audience before our trainings. We've learned when it comes to the DEI space, BIPOC around the country are asking the same questions:

- Why are people so invested in denying the validity of my personal experiences?
- Why are people so convinced that I'm interpreting my life incorrectly when racism keeps hurting me and my family over and over and over again?
- Why is it so hard to get people to realize the struggles that people like me have?

The just world fallacy is one big reason why.

One of the most prevalent signs that someone is basing their opinion on the just world fallacy is victim blaming. This is because, if the world is fair, the only way to justify the misfortune of others is by creating a narrative where they, for some reason, deserve what happened to them. The other side of the just-world-fallacy coin is that the reason good things happen to certain people is that those people have done something to deserve it. As it relates to race, this quickly becomes problematic. Equity issues tend to be structural in nature, and a belief that outcomes, good and bad, are deserved fails to take into account the complex societal circumstances that affect those outcomes. This in turn precludes problem solving on the structural level.

Antidote to the Just World Fallacy: Flip the Script

Whenever we have gaps in our understanding, we fill those gaps with assumptions; when we fall prey to the just world fallacy, those assumptions are ones consistent with the belief that the world is fair. Countering this requires identifying what our assumptions are, and what other information they may be keeping us from seeing.

To do this, ask yourself two simple questions:

- *What story am I telling myself?* This will help you to draw out any potentially unfair or inaccurate assumptions that are coloring your perspective.
- *What are possible alternative explanations that I haven't considered?* This helps us understand that our assumptions may be no more valid than possible alternatives.

Let's revisit that example of racial inequity in schools, and the idea that any student who has a subpar outcome must not be working hard enough. The story you're telling yourself here is: *Students deserve to be in their current position. Any disparate educational outcomes are the student's fault. If a Black student isn't doing as well as a White student, then it's because they aren't working as hard. Nothing needs to change other than their mindset.*

Flipping the script means considering other potential explanations—here, factors *outside* of students' control that could impact their performance, like housing instability or food insecurity.

Will asking yourself these questions always give you the "right" answer? No. However, they will help you see where you might be wrong and trigger the requisite curiosity for further analysis. In other words, when we embrace the idea that we might be getting it wrong, it makes it more likely that we'll get it right.

MORAL LICENSING

Why are you more likely to eat unhealthy food after a good workout? *Moral licensing* may be the answer. With moral licensing, doing something good gives us a "license" to do something bad. Essentially, if we have done well in the past, then it gives us an excuse for not doing well, or not doing more, in the present.[16]

Often in discussions about race, people say things like, "Stop being so negative. Look how far we've come as a country!" or, my personal favorite, "A Black person from the year 1900 wouldn't even consider what's happening today to be racist." First of all, whether or not this unnamed Black person who is more than 120 years old would consider something racist is an odd standard—but I digress. Second, focusing on how things were worse in the past is a distraction from the real issue: the work that needs to be done now.

Moral licensing has a significant impact on issues of equity. According to one study, "people are more willing to express attitudes that could be viewed as prejudiced when their past behavior has established their credentials as non-prejudiced persons."[17] In other words, when a person feels as though they've already done something positive as it relates to race and equity in the past, it may actually *decrease* the likelihood of them making more positive strides in the future.

Note that because organizations are made up of individuals who are susceptible to this phenomenon, they too can suffer from the effects of moral licensing. Companies can feel as though they've already *done enough* on an organizational level to promote racial equity and, as a result, have a moral license to not take additional steps forward or continue to invest in future programs.

Antidote for Moral Licensing: Acknowledge the Gains but Focus on the Current Pains

Comments on how far we've come as a country—or how far your workplace has come—are usually well intentioned, designed to make the people listening feel better about the current circumstances. However, these comments aren't harmless, because of the cover they provide for moral licensing.

While you might be tempted to just dismiss a comment about past gains as irrelevant, denying its validity often makes the other person more fixated on conveying their point. Instead, acknowledge it briefly and then hop back on the conversational highway. I might respond with something like, "I agree with you; it's very impressive how far we've come as a society. The racism of today looks nothing like the racism of the past, and we should all be grateful for that. At the same time, we shouldn't be complacent either. There are still some significant issues for us to address, like . . ." That allows you to refocus the conversation in a more productive direction.

As author and motivational speaker Tony Robbins has noted, "Change happens when the pain of staying the same is greater than the pain of change." If people feel too good about where they are as it relates to racial equity, they won't have the requisite motivation to work for change. So, as much as we want to focus on the positive, we need to make sure that we're not risking complacency. Don't let past wins interfere with the prospect of future ones.

THE GREAT PAIN-OFF

As we've seen, in difficult conversations about race, emotions can run high. Validating other people's emotions is important, both for you and your conversation partner. But when one person's goal in the conversation is not improving mutual understanding and problem solving but rather finding catharsis, it can make difficult conversations harder.

According to the American Psychological Association, *catharsis* is "the release of strong, pent-up emotions."[18] In the right settings, catharsis can be a productive way to process strong emotions.[19]

However, in difficult conversations, where emotions are already running high, a person who is experiencing emotional pain sometimes seeks catharsis by either venting their emotions or, consciously or subconsciously, trying to inflict pain on the other person. This is problematic because, rather than being a mutual exchange of ideas, the conversation becomes a punitive emotional release. Releasing those negative emotions might make a person feel better initially, but it is likely to take the conversation in an unproductive direction while permanently damaging the relationship.

A common variation of cathartic persuasion is what I like to call a "pain-off." It's like two elderly friends bickering about who has the worst physical ailments, or two college students competing over who got the least amount of sleep from studying the night before: a type of emotional one-upping: "I've had it worse than you have, so my position is more valid."

Let's say you're having a conversation about privilege and a Latinx colleague shares how race has affected their life and the lives of their friends and family members. Then a White colleague immediately responds by saying, "Well, my mother raised all four of my siblings by herself and we were living in poverty throughout my childhood and we still made it."

What often follows is an unproductive conversation about which scenario is worse and why. Instead of approaching the conversation in a way that honors and accepts each other's lived experiences, they instead try to use their past pains to *invalidate* each other's experiences.

We all have emotional struggles, and those struggles are all valid. But when discussing past hurts, there needs to be a level of emotional restraint. Escalating discussions over whose pain is worse only get us further away from productive dialogue.

Antidote for the Great Pain-Off, Part 1: Break the Pain-Off Cycle Using the Right Kind of Empathy

It is tough to be empathetic when you are hurting, and showing empathy to those who are causing you emotional distress is not a natural thing to do. But empathy is the most effective way to prevent a pain-off from getting out of control.

Everywhere you turn, some "expert" is telling you to empathize. And I apologize in advance, because I'm going to do the same. But before I do, I want to *empathize* with you, because empathizing is hard to do, and our psychology makes it even harder.

To understand this, let's break empathy up into two different types, *psychological empathy* and *intentional empathy*. Intentional empathy is a choice you make to understand what your conversational partner sees, thinks, and feels about the situation. Psychological empathy, on the other hand, is not a choice; it's a psychological reality. Most of the well-meaning advice to empathize neither makes this distinction nor considers an important scientifically demonstrated reality: that our ability to empathize is influenced by ingroup bias. Studies have shown that it's easier for us to empathize with people who we perceive to be on the same team. Other research has demonstrated that it is simply more difficult to empathize with those who are of different races and ethnicities.[20]

Imagine you're watching a contact sport, such as American football, and you are rooting for a specific team. What happens when the other team's linebacker blasts your team's quarterback at full speed, dislocating his throwing shoulder? You cringe and maybe even reflexively hold your own shoulder. This is because when somebody on your team is hurt, it's almost like you are being hurt—you feel their pain. If the injured player is on the opposing team, you are less likely to experience that same sympathetic reaction.

This is why the superficial advice to be empathetic in these kinds of situations is doomed to fail. It's insufficient. It fails to factor in that, due to ingroup and outgroup bias, it is more challenging for us to empathize with people who we don't readily perceive to be part of our ingroup.

If you're in a conversation with someone who's different from you—whether racially, ideologically, or otherwise—you can't rely on psychological empathy. You have to rely on intentional empathy. In the middle of a pain-off, you have to suspend judgment and try to fully understand the other person's story *from their perspective*.

- What do they see or perceive?
- How is their perspective influencing how they feel?
- How does their perspective influence how they think about the situation?

Understanding the other person's perspective, to be clear, does not mean that you need to agree with their ultimate conclusion. But it will help you understand where they're coming from, which will help you adjust your approach as the conversation develops.

Maximizing Psychological Empathy—Same Team, Same Goals

While psychological empathy is not a choice the way intentional empathy is, you can still trigger psychological empathy even when it doesn't happen naturally by intentionally pointing out similarities between you and the person you're speaking with. Doing so will help you both overcome unconscious biases against each other, and allow you to avail yourself of the relationship benefits of the ingroup.

Affinity bias is the tendency to prefer people who are like you. When it comes to hiring and company inclusion efforts, this bias is highly problematic because it can lead to the hiring and promotion only of people who "fit": who are White if the senior staff and hiring manager are White, for example, or who came from the same alma mater. However, in one-on-one conversations, it is a critical element of building rapport. Do you both have kids? Did you go to the same school? Do you watch the same shows? Find points of similarity and point them out.

Several studies have shown consistent bias in healthcare against Black, Latinx, and other "dark-skinned" patients.[21] Knowing this, back when Whitney was pregnant and I would accompany her to her maternity wellness checks, I would always find a way to casually mention that Whitney is a doctor. The doctors' and nurses' eyes would always light up and they would begin asking questions: "Oh, where do you practice? Do you know so-and-so?" As soon as they knew they were talking to a fellow medical professional, their whole demeanor changed and they treated Whitney a lot better. We didn't know whether or not she was going to be treated unfairly, but we minimized the likelihood that she would be by clearly demonstrating similarity.

Allan Tsang is a negotiation coach who counsels businesses negotiating multimillion-dollar deals. He was born in Hong Kong, raised in Ghana, and now lives in the Appalachian South. As part of his work, he's experienced both microaggressions and macroaggressions. "In Asia," he told me, "everyone looks more or less similar, so you are initially accepted and then they start to differentiate as they get to know you. In the United States, initially they won't accept you if you look different, but as they get to know you, they begin to accept you." To overcome this, he is intentional about uncovering shared values and core beliefs early on. The more he does this, the more he's found others embrace him as one of their own.

Another way to establish similarity during a conversation, and in turn trigger mutual affinity and empathy, is by pointing out where you agree. Even in the most difficult of conversations, there will be something the other person says that you can agree with, and in my experience, saying that I agree with their valid points makes it more likely they will feel comfortable doing the same.

If you are able to see each other as on the same team and having the same goals—if you see each other as collaborators rather than combatants—it is much more likely that you'll have a productive conversation.

Antidote for the Great Pain-Off, Part 2: Avoid Comparing Stories

A lot of times a pain-off is accidental. When we hear someone else's story, in order to understand it, we often filter it through our own stories or other stories we're already familiar with. We share our own, similar stories in an attempt to connect.

The problem with this is twofold. First, we haven't lived anyone else's experiences, so it's impossible for us to *fully* understand what they went through. As a first-generation Caribbean American, my experience in America will be different from that of a first-generation German American, which will be different from that of a first-generation Chinese American, and so forth—even though, as first-generation immigrants, we may have certain things in common. By inserting our story into the mix, and relying on our story for understanding rather than focusing on the other person's story as unique and independent of our own, we may overestimate our ability to understand where they're coming from.

Second, sharing our stories doesn't always improve the quality of the conversation. The strategic value of using our stories to understand another person's is frequently more personal than interpersonal. A similar story that comes to our mind can be a great starting point for our understanding. Then we can use our curiosity to learn more about the other person's story and deepen our understanding. But sharing our story is not always helpful for that other person. We need to ask ourselves how sharing our story is likely to be perceived. Will the other person find it valuable, or will it communicate that you believe you understand their experience fully, when you don't? Will the other person feel as if we are trying to "one-up" them—as if we believe our experience was worse or more important? They may see this as invalidating what they have shared, and they may respond by emphasizing the differences between their experience and our own. Because of this, when stories are used inappropriately, they can actually pull us apart rather than bring us together.

There are undoubtedly times where an exchange of stories is helpful. We just need to be mindful of when and how we insert our stories into the conversation.

In my own difficult conversations, I've noticed an interesting trend. The more emotional I am, the more right I feel, and, in many cases, the more right I feel, the more incorrect I am. When you're emotional, your biases take over. You start to see your conversational partner as the enemy and stop considering things objectively or communicating collaboratively. They'll pick up on that and reciprocate, which is when things can spiral out of control.

As we've seen with the power of empathy, however, triggering the *right* emotions can also help us see where we're wrong. They can help overcome biases, and lead to more productive conversations.

You've learned a handful of strategies in this chapter for managing our shared psychological tendencies and combating specific biases. In part two, you'll learn even more—and more concrete—strategies to ensure your difficult conversations about race are more productive, less frustrating, and more likely to lead to the positive outcomes you want.

DISCUSSION QUESTIONS

- Can you identify instances when you have thought or acted a certain way because of an implicit bias?
- Are there elements of your identity that you felt were indirectly attacked during a past difficult conversation?
- After reading this chapter, what can you do differently to make sure biases aren't inappropriately impacting how you communicate and connect with others?

PART
TWO

The Solution

CHAPTER
FOUR

THE ART OF STRATEGY

The goal of part one was to address some of the psychological and personal challenges that can make conversations about race so difficult. Now that you have an understanding of these challenges, we can discuss how to approach these conversations in a way that's productive, not destructive.

THINKING STRATEGICALLY

I mentioned in the introduction that to be effective in conversations about race, it's critical to be outcome oriented—to understand what you're trying to accomplish. Only then can you be strategic about reaching that goal.

Strategy, most simply, is a plan that helps you win. *But, Kwame,* you might be thinking, *you just said we should avoid these conversations becoming adversarial!* That's true; I did. "Winning" in the case of these conversations shouldn't be seen as a competitive, "me versus you" type of altercation. Here, "winning" is about your goals for the conversation. For me, I'm winning if I'm moving toward my ultimate goal and if we're able to deepen our mutual understanding—if the conversation ends with me and my conversation partner knowing more than when we began.

What is winning for you? Do you want to change hearts and minds? Do you want to avoid offending the other person and leave the conversation with your relationship intact? Do you want to solve a problem? Do you want to vent? Different conversations have different goals, and each of these is legitimate in its own way. The most important thing is to identify *your* goal in a given conversation, because once you do, you can make a plan for how to achieve it.

Ultimately, this is what strategy comes down to: a plan for moving a conversation toward your goal, without inviting unnecessary resistance from the other person. Everything that you say, or do *not* say, should move you toward your ultimate goal.

It's easy to get distracted in conversations about race because they are emotional and complex. To succeed, you need to strategically focus on what is within your control, while acknowledging and accounting for things that are outside of your control. This includes:

- past events.
- the emotions, opinions, beliefs, and actions of other people.
- the conditions of your birth (race, religious upbringing, socioeconomic status).

Here, in contrast, is what *is* within your control:

- your mindset.
- your strategy.
- what you do.
- what you say.
- how you say it.

One of my favorite things to do in my free time is play chess; I've played over nineteen thousand games on chess.com. (I hope you think that's cool; when I tell Whitney about it, she certainly doesn't.) Chess is all about strategically moving your pieces around the board to put them in the best position for you to win the game. Conversations are the same: they're all about strategically choosing your words to put yourself in the best position to succeed.

When I'm playing chess, it's easy to get distracted and focus on things that are not in my current control—for example, beating myself up for a past bad move, or thinking about how annoying it is when my opponent makes certain kinds of moves. But that doesn't help me perform at a higher level in the moment. What I do to stay focused is ask myself, "What is the best move I can make given my current position?"

You can ask yourself the same question in these conversations. All you can do at any given moment is the best you can do. There's little value in wasting your cognitive energy contemplating things outside of your control.

To strategize effectively, you also need to do your homework. It's hard to know how to get where you're going if you don't have a map. Many people go into difficult conversations about race by freestyling and hoping for the best. But hope is not a strategy. Thoroughly preparing before the conversation will help you understand what to do and say and what barriers you need to overcome, then guide you once the conversation begins.

In the American Negotiation Institute's negotiation trainings, we always emphasize the importance of *active* preparation. Over the years, I've seen an increasing amount of resistance to this call for preparation. It's not that people don't believe in its importance; rather, they tell me, they feel like they have no time to do it. In response, we put together guides to help our clients prepare for various kinds of difficult conversations. If you go to www.amer-icannegotiationinstitute.com/negotiation-guides, you can access our free guides—including, of course, one specifically designed to help you prepare for difficult conversations about race at work.* Tens of thousands of people have used these free guides to improve their performance in their difficult conversations; they're the easiest way for you to plan and strategize for these conversations.

---

* You can also access guides on how to negotiate your salary and how to negotiate your next car purchase.

But let's say you don't even have time to use the guide. What do you do? Ask yourself three questions:

- What do I hope to accomplish in this conversation?
- Given what I know about them and the situation, what is likely to be their goal?
- What are three questions I can ask them that will help me to understand their position?

Answering them takes less than a minute and will help you feel a lot more confident going into the conversation.

For the rest of the chapter we're going to focus on the key strategic considerations to keep in mind for making these conversations easier. The first half of the chapter focuses on how to build a firm foundation for a constructive conversation and strong working relationship with your conversation partner. Your message is like a seed. It needs to be planted in receptive and fertile soil. You may have a powerful message, but if the listener isn't receptive, whether because of your relationship with them or how you've approached the conversation, your message will have minimal or, even worse, negative impact.

The second half of the chapter consists of practical tools that you can use during the conversation to accomplish your specific goals. This is the part that will help you know what to say and how to say it.

While there's nothing that you can do to guarantee success, there is plenty that you can do to increase your likelihood of succeeding. After reading this chapter you'll have a set of powerful and practical tools to use in your next difficult conversation about race.

NEVER COMPROMISE YOUR CORE VALUES OR ACCEPT MISTREATMENT

Before we get to the strategies themselves, it's important to stress one thing: no matter what your strategy is, you should never compromise your core values or accept mistreatment.

Whenever we conduct negotiation trainings, we always start by asking, "What is negotiation?" Inevitably someone says, "Compromise."

But here's a secret: not all negotiation requires compromise and, most importantly, there are certain things you should never compromise, like your safety or your core values. Also, no legitimate negotiation strategy includes accepting racial abuse.

Rebecca Zung, an attorney, negotiation expert, and author of the best-selling book *Negotiate Like YOU M.A.T.T.E.R.*, writes, "The 'M' in the acronym stands for my value is defined by me because all humans have the same needs, which are to be seen, heard, and know that they matter." We all need to feel acknowledged and respected. And any conversation or solution that doesn't respect you or your values isn't one you should accept.

Don't be afraid to draw lines to keep yourself safe. All you need to say is, "I'm not comfortable with what's happening right now. I think it would be best to end the conversation here." Then, you can revisit the discussion if and when it becomes appropriate. Don't feel forced to continue if the compromise the other person is asking for feels inappropriate (for example, if you have a past experience of racial trauma and people are pushing you to share when you don't feel comfortable doing so). Remember, if you need the conversation to end, it ends.

To be clear, this is not the same as intellectual rigidity. Although your core values stay the same, your perspective can change. For example, you may believe that everyone should be treated fairly and that anything that doesn't treat people the exact same way is unfair. That core value may lead you to believe that diverse hiring initiatives are unfair to White people. However, if you view things from a different perspective, you might come to believe that your company inadvertently but unfairly favored the hiring of White candidates because of how its selection process is structured. This would shift your perspective on diverse hiring programs without compromising your core value of fairness.

The distinction between your core values and your current (potentially limited) perspective is often hard to see. It might take some introspection to determine where that line should be drawn. The important thing to remember here is that respect and safety are critical to having these crucial conversations about race—and that means *you* feel safe and respected, too.

BEGIN BY BUILDING TRUST

Psychologically speaking, there's a lot working against you in these conversations. As you saw in chapter three, biases have a significant impact on both a conversation's process and outcome. This isn't news, really; it's why bias training exists. But many bias trainings are limited because they focus only on what you as an individual can do to overcome your biases. They very often fail to offer solutions for how to overcome bias in other people.

I see the biases of others not as an insurmountable obstacle but an additional strategic consideration. What I mean by this is that I consider how bias may impact each interaction, and then determine what positive biases I can use to overcome it.

I'm not willing to simply accept a position of powerlessness in the conversation by saying there's nothing I can do to overcome these psychological challenges. I'm not going to put the responsibility of productive dialogue in the hands of someone else. Although you can't control others' psychological response, you can influence their response with your strategic approach.

This will come as no surprise, but telling the person you're talking to, "I think you're being biased" probably won't work. Remember, bias is largely subconscious, which means the person likely doesn't realize it's there. Instead, overcoming biases in others requires subtlety. It means targeting their subconscious by building trust.

Think about somebody you know: your mom, your best friend, a coworker. If I were to ask you whether or not you trust them, how long would it take for you to answer?

You should be able to make that assessment almost instantly, without deep thought. That's why I see trust in a way that may be considered controversial: *trust is a positive bias*. Moreover, it's a positive bias that gives you significant benefits in these conversations. If your conversation partner trusts you, they are more likely to:

- *Be vulnerable*. They will be more open to sharing how they see, think, and feel, leading to more meaningful engagement.
- *Be persuadable*. They'll be more willing to agree with what you say.
- *Be less critical*. They'll be less skeptical and less likely to engage in reflexive rejection.
- *Assume positive intent*. They'll be more likely to interpret any ambiguities favorably.

Trust is key. If the other person doesn't see you as someone on their team, it will be more difficult for them to hear and empathize with you. This will make it harder for you to connect and persuade. To gain that kind of trust, we need to approach our conversations in ways that make it more likely for the other person to see us as part of their ingroup instead of an outgroup.

There are things you can do during a conversation to increase the likelihood that the other person will see you as on their own team (see "Maximizing Psychological Empathy—Same Team, Same Goals" in the previous chapter), but real trust takes time. If you're only trying to build trust with the person *after* the difficult conversation begins, then you're going to struggle. You need to find a way to have positive interactions with people *before* you speak with them. The psychology of the mere exposure effect can offer insight as to why this works: the more you're exposed to something in a positive way, the more you like it.

Each interaction you have with another person is, at minimum, an opportunity to invest in what I like to call your "relationship bank account." With each positive interaction, you are increasing how much goodwill they feel toward you and building a strong working relationship that is typified by trust.

One of people's biggest fears when it comes to conversations on the topic of DEI is saying or doing something offensive. As I mentioned earlier, you will certainly make mistakes, and say or do something offensive, because these conversations are complex. However, creating a trusting relationship is one of the best ways to prevent the negative consequences we fear will result from these inevitable mistakes. Stronger relationships make it easier for others to forgive, easier for them to treat you with grace and assume positive intent, and more likely that they will feel comfortable enough with you to let you know when you've messed up without completely writing off the relationship.

Code Switching

While building trust is best done over time, one additional strategy you can use during a conversation to create a sense of trust quickly is *code switching*, a somewhat controversial component of cultural intelligence.

Mark Davis is a lawyer and negotiation expert who specializes in cultural intelligence (CQ). He explains CQ as what helps you to understand "when to adapt and when not to adapt [y]our style, approach, or strategy."[1] In his trainings for ANI, he helps people recognize how increasing their CQ can help professionals better understand, empathize with, connect to, and persuade others. According to the *Harvard Business Review*, one of the benefits of CQ is that it helps you "to make sense of unfamiliar contexts and then blend in."[2]

Code switching is "the practice of shifting the languages you use or the way you express yourself in your conversations,"[3] usually in order to blend in with whoever you are speaking to. This can come in many forms; for example, it might take the form of a slight shift in the way you speak or the cultural references and stories you use to convey meaning. Some people view code switching as a useful skill that allows you to speak different cultural dialects, while others see it (when BIPOC use it to sound more like the White majority) as assimilating with a dominant culture that refuses to accept you for who you are. Like most things, the truth lies somewhere in between the extremes.

One time, I was talking to a Black friend about the pros and cons of code switching, and he said, "Hard pass. I'm not shuckin' and jivin' for White people. Code switching is selling out. I refuse to do it."

Then I said, "You know I'm code switching for you right now, right?"

"What?"

"This is my African American accent. It's not the one I grew up with. But I've never really *chosen* to code switch. It happens naturally the more time I spend with people."

When I was growing up in Tiffin, people would say I sounded like I was from the Caribbean. When I visited family in the Caribbean, they'd say I sounded American. But, over time, I learned to adapt and flow as necessary in different contexts with different people. Then when I went to college and spent time with American Black people, they said I sounded White—but the more time I spent with them, the more I began to speak the way they did.

We all code switch to a certain extent. It's why you can be completely authentic when talking to your kids, partner, colleagues at work, parents, and best friends while sounding completely different in each of those conversations. The problem isn't with whether or not people code switch, it's when they feel as though they have to. Unfortunately, BIPOC often feel they *need* to code switch to be accepted and understood by their colleagues at work.

In the growing field of cultural intelligence, code switching is considered a type of *mimicry*, and can be incredibly effective in overcoming others' negative bias by making it easier for them to trust you. However, it only works if you have intimate knowledge and appreciation of the culture that you find yourself in. If you try to use it without knowing the culture, your mimicry likely will be perceived as mockery, which is highly problematic and will quickly erode goodwill.[4]

For me, when it comes to code switching, I don't know how *not* to do it. It sounds odd, but for my unique life experience, this fluid adaptation is my form of authentic self-expression. I've spent sizable amounts of time with people of different backgrounds, and so there is a true, authentic version of Kwame for each of them. But, if I'm not intimately familiar with a culture, I won't try to code switch because it would be inauthentic and ultimately do more harm than good.

Jason Christie is a successful Afro-Caribbean real estate broker and the leader of the Polaris Team in New York City. In his episode of ANI's podcast, *Negotiate Anything*,[5] he calls code switching his superpower. In a single day, Jason could be speaking Mandarin, courting Wall Street investors, negotiating deals with Hasidic Jews, and then getting drinks with friends in Harlem. Regardless of the environment, he knows how to speak the language, figuratively and literally, and that's often what lets him close deals others can't.

On the podcast, he shares a story about an open house he held in an apartment where a Chinese woman wanted to talk with him. They were able to chat briefly, which is when he learned she was from China, but he had other clients he needed to speak with, too. Still, he wanted to make sure she felt seen and valued, so he said to her in Mandarin, "Don't worry. We can chat later. I'm here for you." This helped him establish trust and build rapport. Her eyes lit up immediately, and later, when they talked, not only did he answer her real estate questions, they also discussed how he knew Mandarin. This connection helped to close the deal. In this situation, Jason was able to code switch *authentically and respectfully* because, after living in Taiwan for more than three years and spending some time in China, he was familiar with the culture.

In your difficult conversations about race, if you're familiar enough with the other person's culture to code switch (something you're likely doing already without conscious intention), they're more likely to see you as like themselves, and that goes a long way toward combating negative bias and building trust. However, if you feel as though code switching would mean compromising key aspects of yourself, then don't do it. Code switching is just one of many potential tools to encourage connection and rapport.

START WITH "LEVEL ONE" COMMUNICATION

When it comes to communication, there are two levels, which I have aptly named *level one communication* and *level two communication*. With level one communication, you're seeking to understand the other person and the situation in order to maintain and strengthen the relationship. In level two communication, you're seeking to persuade in order to change behaviors or beliefs.

Trust is one important foundation that can make difficult conversations easier. Another is understanding which of these two types of communication to begin with. Sequence matters. Difficult conversations often begin—and quickly end—with level two communication because people try to persuade others before taking the time to understand them. But the levels of communication are named level one and level two for a reason. We always start in level one.

Level One Communication

A major part of level one communication is to try, as much as possible, to exit the conversation without doing or receiving damage, so that you maintain the relationship. Particularly in an office environment, you and your conversation partner likely will need to continue working together. Using level one communication makes it easier for both of you to meaningfully engage without becoming combative and jeopardizing the relationship.

In level one communication, your goals are simple:

1. *Learn, don't teach.* Lead with curiosity to get a better understanding of the other person's perspective. Seek to understand before asking to be understood; ask questions, listen, and then ask more questions to clarify your understanding.

2. *Share, don't preach.* Share your perspective as a humble observation rather than a gospel truth. (Remember the six blind men and the elephant?) Also, when others sense arrogance or moral superiority in your message, they will resist hearing it. No one likes to feel inferior.

3. *Respect despite differences.* You won't always agree with what the other person says, but agreement isn't the point (at least at this conversation level). Respect here is shown through nonjudgmental listening.

Listening is often the hardest part of the conversation, particularly listening nonjudgmentally without jumping in and "correcting" people where you disagree. But in my opinion, listening is even *more* important when you don't agree. Level one communication is the easiest: you want to understand how the other person sees, thinks, and feels about the situation, in order to empathize with them. Empathy does not mean agreement; it just means understanding. It's not about truth, it's about perspective. And remember: it's harder to empathize when you disagree.

This is where the intentional empathy we talked about in the last chapter comes into play.

Listening in conversations about race can be especially difficult; people put their defenses up early. When you take the time to listen, it makes it more likely that the other person will reciprocate. In other words, when you listen, the chances that you will be heard improve.

Still, as much as you want and need to empathize, there are limits to our empathy. When my wife was in the hospital delivering our second son, I knew she was uncomfortable and in pain, but I couldn't fully empathize because I've never had the experience of being pregnant and never will. The same will be true in some of your conversations, especially about race, no matter how well you listen. And that's okay. Listen and learn with the goal of understanding the other person as much as you can, but with the knowledge that your understanding will always be incomplete.

Empathy in level one conversations is not only a way to show you care about the other person and maintain the relationship. It's also a strategic choice—especially when your goal is to not only understand, but persuade. Imagine playing chess and refusing to consider what move the other side made and why they made it. It would be putting yourself at a strategic disadvantage. Level one communication is the foundation for level two communication.

Remember this important point: *Empathy is not a concession, it's a necessary part of persuasion.* I recommend approaching these conversations with the belief that you have to earn the right to persuade the other person. If the person you're speaking with doesn't believe you fully understand where they're coming from, then in their mind you haven't earned the right to say that they are wrong.

Level Two Communication

Sometimes, level one communication is also where we end—for example, if our conversational goal is to simply share perspectives or understand a situation, rather than solve a specific problem. However, if we want to change hearts and minds, then we have to move to level two.

Level two communication frequently happens organically. The mutual understanding you fostered in level one means the other person now has a better understanding of *your* perspective and may adjust their position on their own. Let's revisit the conversation from last chapter about academic performance in schools. In that example, starting the conversation by getting a better understanding of their perspective and asking questions to gauge their familiarity with the funding scheme of public education may have been all they needed to recognize that their initial analysis—which failed to account for structural considerations—was incomplete, and to adjust their position accordingly.

However, persuasion doesn't always happen organically through level one communication. If you've achieved greater mutual understanding but you still haven't solved the problem you wanted to solve, you may need to push the conversation a little bit further. This is where the other strategies in this chapter and the rest of the book come into play.

ESTABLISH A COLLABORATIVE CONVERSATIONAL FRAME

Everyone comes to a conversation with a particular framing in mind: a story that impacts the way we see ourselves, the other person, and the goal of the conversation. Many times, especially in conversations on sensitive topics such as race, that story is a classic hero-versus-villain story where we're the hero and the other person is the villain. However, they are coming into the conversation with their own story, where, unfortunately, *you* may be playing the role of the villain.

One of the most important parts of starting a difficult conversation is framing it in a way that will help you achieve your goals—one that is collaborative rather than combative, where the two of you are the heroes and the problem is the villain. When I have a conversation, I don't want it to feel like me versus you; instead, it's me *and* you versus the problem.

When you're beginning a conversation, you want to frame it using what I call "yes-able propositions": positive, collaborative, and aspirational statements that the other person can easily lean into and agree with. This helps create positive momentum for the conversation, in addition to ensuring you're both on the same page about the conversation's goals and your roles in it.

As a lawyer, I find framing things this way to be challenging because our legal system is actually designed to be adversarial. However, my negotiations are more productive if I discover a way to frame my interactions with opposing counsel collaboratively. For example, I'll start off the negotiation by saying something like this to the other lawyer: "I know our clients have been dealing with this situation for a while. I'm looking forward to working with you to figure out a way for both of them to move forward and put this behind them." Taking the time to frame the conversation in terms of *working with* versus *working against* does wonders when it comes to circumventing needless resistance.

When talking about race at work, it should be easier to frame things collaboratively because, if you're in the same company, you are ostensibly already collaborators—you are on the same company team. Let's say you're discussing the creation of a new DEI initiative at work, but you've been having trouble convincing someone on the committee of the importance of training that will ensure employees have the skills they need to collaborate and communicate effectively in the modern workplace. You can say something like, "I think we have a great opportunity to create a program that matches our mission, vision, and values, and I'd like to chat with you about what we can do to approach this in a way that moves our company in the right direction." Instead of framing the conversation as adversarial, where you and the other person are at odds—something that invites more resistance, because they can feel the negativity in your approach—you are framing it in a way that makes it more likely for the other person to meaningfully engage.

When you begin by framing the conversation as collaborative versus combative, you are also employing *conversational leadership,* a strategy in which you model the behavior you want to see in the conversation. It keeps the conversation moving in a productive direction while communicating to your partner what is important and unimportant to the discussion. Productive conversations on sensitive issues rarely happen without one or both partners being intentional about the flow of the discussion.

Situation + Impact + Invitation

One of the hardest parts of any conversation is the beginning, and it can be especially awkward when one of the participants doesn't realize that a conversation on the topic needs to happen. Here's a brief formula you can use to get things started:

$$situation + impact + invitation = engaged\ communication$$

Situation

In this step, you want to describe the situation using what I call "naked facts"—facts that are completely stripped of judgment or interpretation. You're describing things in a way that, no matter what the other person believes about a particular situation, they can at least agree that the situation itself exists or happened. For example, instead of saying, "You made an offensive joke in the meeting yesterday," you would say, "In the meeting yesterday you said [insert direct quote here]."

This helps you dodge early resistance to the conversation. At this point, all you're trying to do is get the person to have a conversation with you on the topic. If you characterize the situation in a way they already disagree with, they may use that as an excuse not to have the conversation at all or begin an argument on an issue that may not even be a core part of the conversation.

Let's say you believe that there are racially inequitable hiring practices at your workplace. Given what we learned about bias and reflexive rejection, consider the difference in how the head of human resources might respond to, "Our hiring process is racist" versus, "A recent applicant reached out to me because they didn't receive a callback when they applied under their own name, but when they applied with the same résumé using a different name, they received a callback within twenty-four hours." They will be more likely to accept the latter than the former.

Impact

In this step, you want to describe the impact of the situation in personal terms. People might disagree with a contention, an argument, or even facts, but it's harder to disagree with your personal evaluation of the effect that something had on you. For example, you would say, "That made me feel uncomfortable because . . . ," "That made me concerned that . . . ," or, "That impacted my work because . . ."

When addressing an issue that is more professional than personal, it may be more beneficial to frame the impact in terms of what's best for the company. For example, you could say, "This will have an impact on our growth because . . . ," or, "This may lead to decreased cohesion and morale because . . ."

Invitation

In the final step, you invite them to have the conversation with you while using a positive frame. You want to make it an invitation, because no one likes feeling ambushed—but you also don't want to give them the opportunity to avoid the conversation entirely. The options here are now or later. If it's a conversation that I believe has to happen, I'm not going to just let someone dodge it by saying I'm talking to the wrong person or this isn't the right time. For example, you might say, "I'd like to talk to you about this soon because . . . ," or "It's important for us to address this as soon as possible because . . . ," or, "Although this may have occurred while you weren't in the office, I still need to talk to you about it because . . ."

Here's an example of what all three steps could look like together:

Situation: "In yesterday's meeting you said, 'XYZ.'"

Impact: "That made me feel really uncomfortable."

Invitation with a positive frame: "I want to have a conversation with you about it because we're going to be working together on this project for the next few months and I think we can do something really great. I want to make sure we can use this conversation as an opportunity to get on the same page."

All three elements are needed for the formula to work. If one of the elements is missing, the other person is likely to feel attacked at the onset of the conversation, and it can be very difficult to recover from that.

ONE PERSON, ONE TOPIC

You will find much more success by following this simple rule: the fewer people involved, the more productive the conversation. Bigger groups are more performative than conversational. People will be more comfortable being open and vulnerable and more likely to adjust their position if they are in a one-on-one conversation, something that, as we saw earlier, is a critical element for the success of these conversations.

Din Jenkins is a former police sergeant and crisis negotiator (current Deputy Chief at Boston Housing Authority) who conducts trainings with ANI. (Needless to say, as a Black police officer, 2020 provided him with frequent opportunities to have difficult conversations about race.) One of the things he consistently finds is "the smaller the audience, the better." It's challenging to have a discussion with multiple people, especially if the subject involves heightened emotions. The dynamics change more rapidly as the size of the group increases, and people tend to form what Din describes as a "pack mentality," where people coalesce along ideological lines and dig their heels in, rather than engage in meaningful communication with the goals of learning, listening, and understanding.

That's why, if a race-related incident occurs in your workplace, instead of bringing the entire staff together to talk about it initially, it makes more strategic sense to begin by talking to each of the affected parties *individually*. The people involved are more likely to open up—and therefore provide you with the information and insights you need to get a more complete understanding of the situation and make better decisions—when speaking one on one than they would be in a group setting.

You should also try to deal with only one issue, or one situation, at a time. Keeping your focus on one issue means that the energy of the meeting stays in one place, and topics don't get conflated and cause needless confusion. For example, let's say you're on a newly formed DEI taskforce in your organization and you've been assigned to address recruitment, retention, training, creating a culture where everyone feels included and as though they belong, and microaggressions in the workplace. Could you imagine trying to cover all of those topics in one forty-five minute meeting about "racial equity"? Yes, all of these issues are related. But each also has its own nuances that require time to tease out. Having the discipline to slow down and address each point thoroughly will increase the quality of conversation. So, as much as possible, simplify the process from the beginning by limiting the scope of discussion and clarifying the issues being discussed.

While many conversations inevitably expand to a series of topics, we can help ensure they remain relevant to the main issue at hand by using the situation + impact + invitation approach. You could start the meeting by saying, "After the recent equity assessment, we discovered that it takes BIPOC employees within our organization, on average, 1.7 years longer to earn a promotion when compared to their White peers with the same qualifications. This means that BIPOC in our organization are missing out on opportunities to advance, which will have a significant impact on their career trajectory and earnings. It also means that we may be exposing our company to potential lawsuits. Considering that this falls under the mandate of the taskforce, and is something that we haven't discussed in past meetings, I think we should focus our time today addressing that issue and what we should do to make things right."

With this introduction, you invite the members to have the discussion in a nonthreatening way, establish what's at stake if the discussion doesn't happen, and clearly set the discussion's parameters. If someone starts to steer the discussion to another issue outside the scope of the meeting, like DEI training, you can then refer back to what you said at the beginning to refocus the conversation on the results of the assessment and what needs to be done to address the issue it brought up.

CALLING OUT VERSUS CALLING IN

Calling out is when you publicly tell someone they have made a racist or otherwise inappropriate comment. An example of calling someone out would be, after they post a questionable meme, you post your unfiltered feelings about the meme's content in the comments for the world to see. Or, after someone says something offensive in a meeting, you might pause the meeting and address that person in front of everyone.

Calling out is often a cathartic form of communication, rather than a persuasive one. It can be more about public shaming than it is about effectively communicating with the person in a way that's likely to lead to change.

When you call someone out, you are mobilizing the pernicious power of shame to tear them down because they think differently from you. This creates a scenario where the other person feels they must defend their honor and fight back. People are unlikely to concede if they have an audience because they're afraid and don't want to lose social standing within the group. This usually leads to reflexive rejection, defensiveness, and shame. The ensuing dialogue can destroy relationships, create enemies instead of allies, and polarize the two parties and onlookers alike.

To avoid the potential strategic challenges of calling someone out, whenever possible, call them *in* instead. Calling in isn't about exposing someone for doing something wrong. It's about sharing your perspective as part of an empathetic dialogue in order to foster learning and create positive change. For example, you might send the person who posted the meme a private message asking to talk about it, or speak with the person who said the offensive thing *after* the meeting, in private, while checking in with your colleagues who may have been offended. Call-ins *decrease* defensiveness by inviting the person in question to the safer space of a one-on-one conversation.

When it comes to difficult conversations about race in the workplace, I'm making two basic assumptions. First, that you want to maintain a decent working relationship with the person you're talking to, while still holding them accountable. Second, that the thing you want to talk to them about isn't something egregious enough to get them fired—just problematic enough to get under your skin and motivate you to initiate a discussion. Assuming both of these are the case, calling them in is your best approach because it decreases the likelihood of reflexive rejection and defensiveness while increasing the likelihood that they will meaningfully engage.

To call someone in, you can start by utilizing the three-step formula from earlier in this chapter for starting a conversation: situation + impact + invitation = engaged communication. You could say something like, "Earlier today you said _____. Some of what you said made me feel uncomfortable. We've been working together for three years and I see you as an important member of our team. I wanted to see if you'd be open to having a conversation with me about it because I'd like to hear your thoughts."

Once you begin the conversation, tell them why what they said was offensive to you. If the issue was a factual matter, have supporting evidence to counter their claim. If their statement was simply offensive or in poor taste, tell them how this made you feel. Then use the Compassionate Curiosity framework in the next chapter to navigate the discussion.

When you've called someone in, it is possible that they will enter the conversation in a defensive position. They're probably in a heightened emotional state and prepared for an argument or a fight. Take the time to create a positive frame for the discussion, as discussed earlier in this chapter when explaining how to make an invitation, and try to increase their comfort so they're more open and receptive.

Your frame should be both positive and collaborative and end with an open-ended question to begin steering the conversation in a productive direction. For example, you could say, "I appreciate you taking the time to chat with me. Like I said in my message, you're an important part of the team and I really enjoy working with you. I want to use this as an opportunity for us to learn from each other. What do you think?" Ending with a question also shows that your goal isn't to lecture them from a place of moral superiority.

One-on-one interactions make it easier for someone to adjust their position. They remove the performative aspect of the interaction and allow both parties to be more vulnerable. And as we've seen, if you can make the other person feel safe, you will greatly increase your likelihood of success.

Many times, when you call someone in, you open up the opportunity to air numerous misconceptions that led to the specific issue you wanted to bring to the other person's attention. You may find out that the person you called in believes that most people think the same way they do, and so your talk could expose the person to new information. The conversation becomes an opportunity for both of you to increase your mutual understanding.

In all of your difficult conversations, remember: the more emotional the conversation, the more personal the communication needs to be. When people are emotional, they are more likely to interpret things negatively, making productive communication harder. Since email, texts, and social media posts carry fewer context clues (e.g., tone or body language) than in-person communication, it's easier for there to be miscommunication due to ambiguity. Whenever possible, have your call-in conversations face to face, via video chat, or over the phone.

KEEP IT SIMPLE AND STAY ON MESSAGE

In psychology, the term *processing fluency* describes how easily a message can be processed. The easier a message is to understand, the more persuasive it is.[6]

Many of you reading this book may have spent time studying race and racism in society. You've probably read the work of academics in the field who bring incredible research data to the table. The challenge I'm guessing you often run into is that when you share the complex, academic points you've learned with colleagues, friends, and family, they do not get it. Coming to these difficult conversations armed with data and statistics and theories isn't enough. You also have to convey the message in a persuasive way. Think of the curse of knowledge we looked at in the last chapter; just because it makes sense to you doesn't mean it will make sense to them.

To be persuasive, you have to think like a marketer. Use the K.I.S.S. method—keep it super simple. Don't use academic terms; use words that everyone can understand.

Think of the rallying cries of the most viral movements of recent memory:

Me Too.
Black Lives Matter.
Make America Great Again.
Yes We Can.

These are all "chantable" phrases. You never hear people chanting academic texts. Keeping your message clear, short, and aspirational will maximize your chances of reaching the person you're addressing.[7]

People are drawn to messages that are not only easy to understand but also comport with their views of the world. It's often not a question of whether something *is* right; it's more a question of whether or not it *feels* right. This is another reason why, when you're having these difficult conversations, especially if you disagree with the other person on a fundamental issue, it's important to increase the fluency of your approach.

With fluency, the more you hear something, the more correct it seems, which is why it is so important to stay on message. Know what you want to say and how you want to say it *before* the conversation begins, then make sure you say it—and after you say it, say it again. When lawyers have a compelling argument, we will repeat it as often as we can to persuade the judge or jury. Although it seems as if the repetition would be boring, we do it because it's incredibly effective.

People often have a fear of repeating themselves, but persistence is part of the persuasive process. It's like marketing. Advertisers want you to hear or see their message over and over and over again, because the more you hear or see it, the more likely you are to buy what they're selling.

This is easier to do when your message is simple. What's the core of what you want to communicate to the other person? Don't feel bad about saying it multiple times during the conversation. For example, if you are a DEI professional, your core message might be, "We need to do what it takes to make everyone feel included." You can find creative ways to say it multiple times throughout the conversation, but don't be afraid of repeating it verbatim. If someone is suggesting an approach that doesn't meet that ideal, ask them, "How would that help us to make everyone feel included?" The more you say it, the more likely it is that others will adopt the phrase as a key metric for success.

SPEAK TO THE HEART, NOT THE HEAD

Where do Mother Teresa and Joseph Stalin agree? Mother Teresa said, "If I look at the mass, I will never act. If I look at the one, I will." Stalin said, "If only one man dies of hunger, that is a tragedy. If millions die, that's only statistics." Data depersonalizes the tragedy behind the numbers. You don't just want people to think; you want them to feel.

There is a lot of research data out there that substantiates the racial inequities we see in society. We like to believe that the data speaks for itself. However, when data speaks by itself, it's often not very persuasive—even when we've taken pains to ensure it is direct and clear. Emotion, on the other hand, is persuasive. That's why blending data with powerful narratives is so effective.

As you present your data, try to also present the story of a sympathetic individual who exemplifies the people behind that data. Don't make it easy for listeners to intellectualize the data and create emotional distance between themselves and the problem at hand. When you give data a name and a face, it becomes much harder to ignore.

ANI works with several public health agencies focused on addressing racial health disparities in infant mortality. For every one thousand Black children born, there are eleven deaths.[8] That's a heartbreaking statistic. But because it's only numbers, it's easier for people to distance themselves emotionally, and so the agencies that hired us often struggled to persuade policy makers and community leaders to take action to address this public health crisis. However, once they focused their message on the death of just one of those babies and shared how it impacted the family, the government officials began to fully grasp the gravity of the situation and started making the changes that the public health professionals recommended.

Rather starting their pitch with a PowerPoint slide filled with statistics, they changed their strategy and chose to start the pitch with a slide that had neither words nor numbers, just an image of a baby sized coffin at a funeral. They said it was the first time they were able to truly get government leaders to commit to taking action.

Decision making is not a logical process; it's a largely emotional exercise that we attempt to rationalize and justify after the fact. We make decisions based on how we feel, and how we feel is often dictated by biases. That's why we need to target our persuasive process, at least partially, toward affecting others' emotions.

ASK QUESTIONS TO BROADEN PERSPECTIVE

When it comes to closely held beliefs, as are often at play during difficult conversations about race, challenging those beliefs directly often leads to reflexive rejection and in some cases will backfire, inadvertently strengthening the position that we want to change. In such cases, a more effective strategy can be to use an epistemological approach to broaden the person's perspective.

Epistemology is the study of knowledge. It addresses how we know what we claim to know. An epistemological approach to persuasion challenges the other person to describe how they know what they know, in an effort to help them see the flaws in their assumptions.[9] The benefit of this approach is that it doesn't require you to be armed with massive numbers of facts or data. This takes pressure off of you because you're not trying to lecture. Instead, you just have to ask the right questions.

This is the approach Daryl Davis used to lead not only former KKK imperial wizard Roger Kelly but more than two hundred other members to leave the group. Notice I said *lead*, not *convince*. He didn't inundate them with facts. He didn't overwhelm them with logic. Instead, he asked questions and was patient. His questions helped them to see the flaws in their thinking, leading them to convince themselves.

To avoid reflexive rejection's power to prevent people from considering different perspectives, I like to ask questions in which the only way to truly answer them is to see things from another perspective. For example, let's go back to the task force scenario from earlier in the chapter, where a company-wide assessment revealed that it takes BIPOC, on average, 1.7 years longer to earn a promotion than their White peers with the same qualifications. You're attempting to persuade the leadership of the organization that this requires further investigation and that changes need to be made, and one of the decision makers, who happens to be a White man, isn't convinced that there's a problem. He says, "You know statistics can lie, right? In my experience, if someone is a hardworking go-getter who does their job, then they get a promotion. If they're not serious about their career or very ambitious, they won't get promotions. It's that simple. I bet if we were to look into it, all of the people who were promoted in a timely manner deserved it and there was a legitimate reason for holding back the rest."

If you happen to disagree with his statements, then it's likely that your stress level began to rise as you read them. What would you say? Keep in mind: *when you lose your cool in a difficult conversation, you give the other person an excuse to stop listening.* I know that when I'm emotional, the first thing I want to say usually isn't the right thing to say. When you feel your emotional temperature starting to rise, slow down and think through what to say next. Let that first thought go by. And if you're still struggling to come up with something productive, try asking an open-ended question about part of their argument. Here, for example, you could ask:

- Have you had any conversations with BIPOC employees in the company about this issue?
- Out of curiosity, what do you mean by "not serious about their career" and "not very ambitious"?
- What do you mean when you say "look into it"? We just hired a company to review the data for us. Can you help me understand why you think you'd find something different?

Asking an open-ended question is also a good idea, because when you're trying to change someone's mind, you want your questions to do more work than your statements. If they adjust their position based on the thoughts your questions inspire, they'll feel as though they changed their mind themselves, not because you told them what to think.

These questions will be difficult for the other person to answer—and that's the point. When people are responding to a situation based on biases, they come up with answers very quickly, as the job of bias is to speed up mental processing by replacing rational thought. Silence, in contrast, indicates that the person is thinking deeply—which is exactly what you want them to do. The worst thing you can do here is ruin the silence by clarifying your question, asking a different question, or saying anything, really. That awkwardness while they're searching deeply within themselves for answers that aren't there is an important part of the process, though the silence can be excruciating for everyone involved. (One of the tricks I use to distract myself from the awkwardness is counting. The longest I've counted while waiting for a response is 120 seconds. Waiting that long was painful but very effective.) Don't ruin a great question by talking through the silence. Let their brains work.

Asking questions culminates in the other person's recognition that they aren't able to answer in a satisfactory manner, which helps them to see the gaps in their understanding. At this point, they usually become more receptive to what you have to say because they'll be looking for help filling in those gaps with legitimate information. (You can now see why it's so important to prepare for your difficult conversations.[10] You won't be nearly as effective if you don't know what you're talking about.)

In the last two examples of open-ended questions, I used some helpful preambles: "Out of curiosity . . ." and "Can you help me understand . . . ?" I use these as question softeners when I'm asking a question that is very direct and could potentially be perceived as aggressive. The less you can trigger the other person's defensiveness, the better.

Here's an example of what this approach could look like within an actual conversation. Let's say you're an Indigenous American and you've been working at an organization for five years. In that time, you've received nearly perfect scores on your reviews. However, four of the people you've trained, all of whom had reviews that were not as good as yours, were promoted over you. You talk to one of your colleagues to get some support and see what you could do about it. However, your colleague seems to keep explaining away the problem without really considering what you're saying—even though they're unfamiliar with the situation.

THEM: It's probably some kind of misunderstanding. Just keep on working hard. I'm sure things will work out the right way.

YOU: I'm not quite sure what you mean by that.

THEM: Well, I'm sure there is some logical explanation for why that is happening.

This is potentially the just world fallacy creeping in. They don't know what's happening but they've already come to the conclusion that the situation is fair because they believe that it should be.

YOU: You said you were sure. How are you sure?

THEM: I don't know, I just feel like racism shouldn't be the first thing that we jump to. It could be thousands of other things.

YOU: How familiar are you with the situation?

THEM: You just told me about it.

YOU: I've been living this for five years, and I've considered lots of different explanations, including it simply being a misunderstanding. Out of curiosity, how can you be sure that race *didn't* play a role in this situation?

THEM: (silence)

Here's another example. Let's say you're a White supervisor of a team in which a White employee committed an infraction and was reprimanded, but continued to work at the company. A few weeks later, a BIPOC team member committed the same infraction and then was fired. One of your fellow managers insinuated during a recent team meeting that your decision was racially motivated and an example of a deep-seated bias against BIPOC in the company. But what they don't know, and what you can't tell them due to the sensitivity of the situation, is that the person of color had received another complaint five weeks earlier that could not be publicly disclosed.

You want to clear the air, so you invite them to have a conversation. You know coming into the conversation that just saying "I'm not racist" will be ineffective, because the response to that will be, "That's exactly what a racist would say!" Instead, you focus on approaching the conversation in a way that meets your goals, which are to learn, understand, repair the relationship, and solve the problem at hand:

YOU: In the meeting today, I felt like you disagreed with my decision—could you share why?

THEM: People should be treated equally and when the White person did this you slapped them on the wrist and when the person of color did the *exact same thing*, you fired them. It's pretty damn clear.

(A note on detours. A conversation is like a highway. If you stay on the highway, you'll make it to your destination, but every once in a while, your conversational partner will create detours that are meant to take you off track. This is a great example of a potential detour. You are going to be tempted to jump in and defend yourself, turning the conversation into an unproductive game of conversational tennis where you make a point and they make a counterpoint and both sides dig in their heels. Instead, stay focused: summarize what you heard, and continue gathering information.)

YOU: Okay, so your perspective is that two people did the exact same thing, and one person was fired because they were a person of color while the other person was able to keep their job because they were White, which isn't fair. Am I understanding that correctly?

THEM: Exactly.

YOU: Okay. I can understand why you're upset about that and it makes sense. Honestly, if I were in your position and I saw what you saw, I would feel the same way. What else is bothering you about this situation?

THEM: I'd say your attitude, if I'm being completely honest. We're dealing with serious acts of racism in this company and it doesn't seem like you're bothered at all. It doesn't seem like anybody is bothered at all. People need to be held accountable for bigotry, including you.

YOU: I see where you're coming from. I agree with you. Acts of racism should not be tolerated. I can tell this is really bothering you, and I can understand why the situation doesn't seem fair. You're somebody I respect, and when you bring something to my attention, I want to always take that seriously. That's why I'm having this conversation with you. If you feel this way, it's likely that other people feel this way too. So, I want to know what I can do to do better.

THEM: You could start by being less racist.

YOU: I'm not going to deny that this looks bad, because it looks absolutely horrible. Here's the problem I'm facing. I want to treat people fairly, and I believe I did that here. My challenge is that, as a manager, there are certain things that I'm required to keep confidential that impacted my decision and, if I'm being completely honest, I don't know how I can justify my decision to you without sharing that confidential information and violating people's privacy. If you were in my shoes, what would you do?

THEM: (silence) I . . . I don't know.

YOU: Yeah, me neither. If there was any way that I could share the information with you, I would. I can't, though, because I'm bound by company policy. I'm not sure who has the authority to give you that information, but the VP over my department might be a good place to start. I respect your desire to get to the bottom of this—I value your opinion of me, and I want to do what I can to earn your trust.

THEM: No, no. I think I jumped the gun. I'm sorry. I appreciate you talking to me through this. It really helped.

Defensiveness isn't an effective strategy *even if that defensiveness is justified*. The only way to defuse complex, emotionally heated situations is by staying engaged, respectful, and curious; asking great questions; and staying collaborative.

HOLD THEM TO THEIR OWN STANDARDS

As you've seen, I'm quite fond of open-ended questions. However, this doesn't mean that closed-ended questions—questions that can only be answered with a restricted set of options, like "yes" or "no"—don't have their place.

I find closed-ended questions to be especially persuasive when they are used to *hold people to their own standards*. According to Stuart Diamond, Wharton Business School professor and author of *Getting More: How You Can Negotiate to Succeed in Work and Life*, "It is a fundamental tenet of human psychology that people hate to contradict themselves. So if you give people a choice between being consistent with their standards—with what they have said and promised previously—and contradicting their standards, people will usually strive to be consistent with their standards."[11]

In the conversation about how it takes BIPOC, on average, 1.7 years longer to earn a promotion when compared to their White peers, using closed-ended questions could look like this:

YOU: Earlier you mentioned that hardworking go-getters who do their jobs will get promotions, right?

THEM: Yes, that's right.

YOU: Okay. Do we want to be the kind of company where hard-working go-getters who do their jobs *don't* get promotions because of their race?

THEM: No! Absolutely not.

YOU: Yeah, me neither. We have this assessment where the data suggests that we might not be living up to that ideal. Now we need to do something about it.

Arguments that hold people to their stated standards are more powerful now than ever. Organizations worldwide have made very bold statements about their commitments to diversity, equity, and inclusion, and you can use these standards that organizations and individuals have set for themselves to bolster your arguments. Persuasion is much easier when you frame a conversation as aiming to help others to live up to the ideals they chose for themselves.

BE HUMBLE

Going into difficult conversations, you want to feel confident—that your position is strong, that you've created an effective strategy, and that you have the skills to execute that strategy. However, you also want to be careful to temper that confidence with humility.

Behaving with *too* much confidence—to the point of being smug or arrogant toward the other person—is off-putting, and can cause your conversation partner to reject *your message* not because they disagree with it, but because your delivery offends them. Humility makes you more persuasive because if you act like you know everything, the other person will look for ways to prove that you don't. We want to avoid approaches that invite resistance.

Arrogance also prevents you from learning. There is no such thing as a fully formed person. We are constantly developing and changing every day of our lives with new experiences and new understanding, and this is as true for you as it is for the person you're talking to. That's why we can't approach these conversations with arrogance or the belief that we are the sole arbiters of truth in the interaction.

One of the most important things for you to do during these conversations is to actively try to find value in the other person's perspective. If you see yourself as somehow intellectually or morally superior to them, then it will be difficult if not impossible to find the validity in what they are saying. Why look for the truth if you believe you already know the answer? Being humble acknowledges that neither side of a difficult conversation knows everything, and that you both have room to learn and grow. After all, if you want someone else to have an open mind in a conversation, you should be willing to have one as well. That means you are willing to change *your* position should the evidence dictate that shift.

Especially when it comes to conversations about race, you want to challenge your own beliefs in the same way you challenge the beliefs of others. At the end of any difficult conversation, both participants should be better for the interaction. If you go in prepared and confident, but still humble and not convinced of your own infallibility, you'll not only be more persuasive, you'll come out of the conversation wiser for it.

Engage, Don't Lecture

Kwame, you might be asking, *how do I approach these conversations with a humble mindset even when I* know *going into the conversation that I'm right?* To begin with, you show humility by remembering you are not right because of who you are, but because the evidence is right. You want your rationale to be so compelling that you can say, "It is not that I want to believe this, it is that I have no choice but to believe this because of . . ."

Keep in mind, however, just because you have facts on your side and figures at the ready does not mean that you should present the other person with a barrage of information, as we saw in "Keep It Simple and Stay on Message." Inundating them with data is not doing either of you any favors. Lecturing the other person as if you are the expert and they are the student, rather than having a true conversation, is a sure way to get them to stop listening.

If you're lecturing rather than conversing, you also might overload your conversation partner without realizing. Do you remember taking a class and becoming lost early in the lecture? With every new point the instructor made, you became increasingly more confused, and there came a point when you felt so far behind the rest of the class that you were afraid to ask the instructor a question. Instead, you threw in the towel, completely disengaging until class ended. If your conversation partner goes into overload, they are unlikely to respond. Their lack of participation in the conversation will frustrate you, and you might wonder why they aren't agreeing with you when all the evidence is right in front of them.

Here is where we need to get back to a humble approach. Take responsibility for the conversation's lackluster performance rather than blaming your conversation partner for their lack of understanding. When you see their eyes starting to glaze over, that's an opportunity to pause and do a comprehension check. Don't ask, "Does that make sense?" because people will rarely admit that they're lost. People want to sound smart, so they'll almost always say yes. Instead, ask, "What are your thoughts on that last point?" Then listen to their response—not only to see if they were following, but also to learn more about their perspective. Conversations are dynamic; they evolve and shift with every word that is said. Giving the other person an opportunity to share helps you understand how and where to adjust your approach as the conversation progresses.

Part of being humble is not being afraid to admit when *we* don't understand something, or when the other person asks a question whose answer we don't know. One of the most powerful phrases you can use in these conversations is, "I don't know." It shows the other person that it's okay to be vulnerable and admit ignorance, and that you are willing to be educated and adjust your position accordingly.

KWAME, I DON'T WANT TO DO ANY OF THIS. IT DOESN'T FEEL RIGHT.

I was conducting a training recently on how to have difficult conversations about race when someone said, "It seems as though we're treating racists with more empathy and respect than the people who are the victims of racists. I'm not interested in accommodating racists. I just want to tell it like it is."

I paused, then responded the way I would in any other difficult conversation. I said, "It sounds like you're frustrated about this approach because there are people who are being victimized and need help, and this approach seems to be focusing more on the emotional needs of the people who are causing the harm."

"Yes, that's right."

"That makes sense. I agree with you. It doesn't seem fair to approach it that way. Especially since your particular focus is the well-being of children. Let me ask you a question. Can you force the people who are causing the problems to change their behavior?"

"What do you mean?"

"Do you have the power by yourself to simply force them to do what you want them to do, or do they still have the free will to do what they want to do?"

"I can't force them to do anything. I wish I could."

"Right, so since you don't have control, you have influence at best. Influence without authority is a lot harder, and it requires a different approach. If you could force them to change, you probably would just do it."

Being empathetic doesn't come naturally to me (when I took the StrengthsFinder test, which ranks your strengths from 1 to 34, my empathy was 34). But intentional empathy is a skill, and I knew I could learn it. With time and practice, I developed the skill and turned it into a conversational habit. A lot of times I don't want to do it. But I know that my ability to empathize impacts my ability to connect, communicate, and persuade.

My legal clients pay me to be effective—not nice. It so happens that the strategies that make me effective—the ones we've been discussing in this chapter—are the same ones that lead to respectful communication. There are times where opposing counsel gets under my skin and I want to lash out, but I know doing so would be putting my emotional desires ahead of the needs of my client.

The strategies I've outlined here certainly aren't for everybody. Ultimately, the right approach comes down to determining what's most important to you—what your goals are—and then selecting strategies that are both authentic to you and put you in the best position to meet those goals. Is your current approach getting you the results that you want? If yes, keep doing it. If not, I hope this book provides you with some useful alternatives.

The strategies in this chapter aren't difficult to understand; they are just difficult to implement. Approaching conversations in this new way will take a lot of discipline because, in many ways, you're fighting against your own psychology. It takes a strong person to be able to display emotional restraint in the face of injustice. Is it fair? No. Is it effective? Yes. Nothing about this process is easy. I'm still working on it, same as you.

This chapter outlined a number of individual strategies you can use in having difficult conversations about race, but in the next chapter, I want to share what is arguably the most powerful conversational approach for race-based discussions: Compassionate Curiosity. It's the approach I use in *all* of my difficult conversations, and it provides a practical framework for employing the strategies we've discussed so far.

DISCUSSION QUESTIONS

- How can you foster conversations with others about sensitive topics in a way that results in a better understanding of their perspective?
- Map out a strategy for having a difficult conversation with someone who you report to at work. Would the way you approach this conversation differ if it was with someone who reports to you? If so, how and why?
- Pick a difficult conversation you foresee having in the near future. Why do you believe it needs to happen? What does "winning" that conversation look like to you, and what strategy or strategies do you need to employ to get there?

CHAPTER
FIVE

MOBILIZING COMPASSIONATE CURIOSITY

Think of having a difficult conversation like sailing a ship through a storm, where the ship is the conversation and the storm is your emotions. It's hard to navigate clearly in the midst of a storm's chaos. Strong emotions can warp your perspective and make it harder to think clearly. What makes the situation even more challenging is that you are not the only person on the boat's deck. You have a conversation partner who is caught in a storm as well. Oftentimes, neither party is at their cognitive best when it matters most.

The key to gaining clarity in the storm of difficult conversations is to use a framework that turns these conversations into something you can predict and prepare for: a framework I call Compassionate Curiosity. I first introduced this framework in my TEDx Talk and first book, *Finding Confidence in Conflict*, and it's designed to help you succeed in your conversations with others, *as well as* in the introspective conversations with yourself that are vital to improving your self-awareness and decision making. It does so by showing you how you can consistently manage both your emotions and the emotions of others in these crucial conversations.

The Compassionate Curiosity framework provides a consistent pathway to productive dialogue that will help you to work through challenges collaboratively with other people, even when you're on opposing sides. It brings order to chaos. No matter how complex and messy the conversation gets, this framework can help you to know what to say and how to say it while increasing the likelihood that you will accomplish your goals without damaging the relationship. Compassionate Curiosity puts you in the best position for success in difficult conversations and makes you a better and more generous conversationalist.

Compassionate Curiosity inspires trust and vulnerability, both of which are incredibly valuable in these difficult conversations. The more someone trusts you, the more information they're willing to share. And the more information you have, the more adept you will be at solving the problem at hand. I can't tell you how many times someone has started a sentence with, "Kwame, I've never told anybody this, but . . ." It is no longer surprising to me when this happens—*even when it is our first conversation*.

The steps of the Compassionate Curiosity framework are simple:

1. Acknowledge and validate emotions.
2. Get curious with compassion.
3. Use joint problem solving.

Just recalling the term *Compassionate Curiosity* on its own will improve your conversational abilities. But the full approach is designed to be easy to remember even during your most difficult conversations.

WHY THIS WORKS

Although the three steps of Compassionate Curiosity are designed to be clear and concise, the framework is based on the complex psychology of emotion and persuasion.

There are two important brain structures to highlight as they relate to emotional regulation: the amygdala and the prefrontal cortex (PFC). Emotions come from the limbic system, of which the amygdala is a crucial part.[1] The amygdala's job is to regulate our emotions and to use them in assessing potential threats. The PFC, on the other hand, is what allows "us to reason and problem solve; understand what we read or hear in a lecture; exercise choice, self-control, and discipline; be creative, and flexibly adjust to change or new information."[2]

When your amygdala perceives a threat, it triggers the body's stress response system. This cognitive process is critical for survival. It's what allows us to respond quickly to threats because it leads to the secretion of adrenaline, which gives us an extra jolt of speed or strength that can help us fight off an attacker or flee to safety.

However, it also impairs the PFC. The PFC is "the brain region that is most sensitive to the detrimental effects of stress exposure," and even mild stress can "cause a rapid and dramatic loss of prefrontal cognitive abilities."[3] This is why it's hard for people to think clearly when they're emotional. It's also why you come up with your best comebacks in the shower—the stress is gone and you're more relaxed.

Strategy is all about making decisions that move you toward your desired outcome. But even if you go into a conversation with a fantastic strategy or strategies, you are going to struggle to implement them if you are unable to control your emotions.

This doesn't mean that emotions aren't an important part of difficult conversations, or that you should avoid feeling or expressing them. People often conflate *emotional challenges* with *emotions*. The two are not the same thing. An emotion only becomes an emotional challenge if it takes you off of the conversational highway.

In fact, when it comes to the person I'm talking to, I'd much rather have them show me their emotions than hide them, because emotions play a critical role in decision making. We act based on what we think *and* feel. If you don't know how someone is feeling, you're flying blind. And if they're feeling particularly frustrated or upset, because of the effect on their PFC, it will be harder for them to think deeply about what you're saying.

My six-year-old son, Kai, and I love playing chess together. In one game, Kai made a mistake and was frustrated. A few moves later, I gave him an opportunity to take my queen, but he didn't see the move because he was *still* frustrated and angry. Then I said, "Kai, stop and think. Show me *all* of the moves your bishop can make." He showed me every move that he could make *except* the one that would give him the advantage. I said, "Kai, there's a move you're missing. I'm going to go to the kitchen and give you some time to think." He sat there staring at the board for more than five minutes and still couldn't see the move. The opportunity was right in front of him but he wasn't able to see it because of his emotional state. He was literally blind with rage.

Remember this important point: it doesn't make sense to send a message to somebody who isn't psychologically ready to receive it. In other words, it doesn't matter how brilliant your point is; the person you're talking to won't be able to process it if they are not in the right mental state. Even if you have all of the data, facts, and statistics on your side, the person still might not accept what you're saying simply because they are not in the proper emotional state to receive and process the message.

The Compassionate Curiosity framework allows you to overcome all of these challenges. When you use this on yourself, it is a tool that allows you to maintain your ability to think and react strategically by helping you manage your own emotions. When used in your conversations with others, it is a tool that helps you to handle others' emotions so the conversation stays productive.

USING COMPASSIONATE CURIOSITY WITH YOURSELF

Let's start with how the Compassionate Curiosity framework can help you manage your own emotions and maintain your strategic focus.

First, I want to acknowledge that using the Compassionate Curiosity framework in conversations with others can come at a cost. In the role of lawyer, mediator, or dealmaker, I often must sacrifice my emotions and ego in order to achieve my goal, because there are points in these difficult conversations where a poorly timed display of emotion would be antithetical to my personal and professional goals.

When we are struggling emotionally, that struggle can manifest in our conversations with others in a number of ways:

- becoming aggressive or hostile.
- shutting down or stonewalling.
- being unable to listen effectively.
- being unable or unwilling to empathize.
- wanting to "win" at the expense of others.
- using shame-based strategies.
- feeling apathetic.

Not surprisingly, these behaviors often take you farther away from your ultimate goals.

The inability to regulate your emotions can lead to a gap between how you *want* to perform and how you *actually* perform in these conversations. You may be thinking, *But, Kwame, I can't just stop myself from having feelings*. That's true. But you can use Compassionate Curiosity to manage them in a manner that's more likely to lead you to the outcomes you seek.

NEGOTIATING WITH YOURSELF

When it comes to these difficult *internal* conversations, I want you to think of yourself as two different people: your strategic self and your emotional self. Strategic Kwame is relentlessly focused on his goals. He wants to do whatever it takes to achieve the objective at hand. Emotional Kwame is very different. He wants to do things that make him feel good or feel better.

The major difference between the two versions of yourself is this: The emotional self is focused on satisfying your desires *in the moment.* The strategic self is focused on satisfying your desires *for the long term.*

For example, if your emotional self gets mad, you may lash out and cause immediate damage in order to satisfy your need for retribution or release. Emotions can overwhelm the rational part of your brain, and as with any mind-altering substance, you are not in complete control when you're under their influence. Once the moment has passed, you look back at what you said or did and are immediately hit with a wave of regret.

Unfortunately, no matter how much you may regret your words or actions, you can't, as they say, put the toothpaste back in the tube. Some mistakes can't be taken back, and that one moment where your emotional self took the wheel may cause irreparable damage to the relationship. That's why emotion management is such a critical part of the process: at the end of the day, if your emotional self dominates your strategic self, you won't be able to put what you've learned from this book into action.

However, you also cannot *deny* your emotions in this process, because they serve an important purpose (one that we will discuss later in the chapter). If you are driving along the conversational highway, think of your emotions as sitting in the car but not having their hands on the wheel. They have input, but not authority. Although both versions of yourself are important, the strategic self must be the one leading the way. Compassionate Curiosity helps you make sure that's the case.

Step 1: Acknowledge and Validate Your Emotions

As much as we might like to, we cannot ignore our emotions. Not only because ignoring them doesn't make them go away, but also because they are extremely valuable. Your emotions provide you with critical information about yourself: your needs, wants, concerns, fears, and much more.

Emotional discomfort is actually a signal that there is something going on that requires further investigation. In order to do that, you need to identify and label the emotion that's at play.

For decades, psychologists have been using an emotional regulation technique called *affect labeling*, in which a person labels their emotions without the "intentional goal of altering emotional responses."[4] Although nothing in the process is *explicitly* geared toward reducing emotional reactivity, the process consistently has a soothing effect. This is because labeling your emotions this way activates a part of the brain called the right ventrolateral prefrontal cortex, which in turn decreases the activity in the amygdala.[5] In other words, when it comes to strong emotions, "name it to tame it."[6] As a result, you'll feel calmer and better able to focus on your goals.

Also, recognize that your emotions are valid—you have a right to feel how you feel. You're a human, and humans have emotions. This is something I struggled with for years. I always wanted to be that strong, stoic Caribbean male. I never felt comfortable acknowledging my emotions and spent decades denying their existence. Once I started honoring the full range of my emotional experience, it was liberating. And by opening myself up to my emotions, allowing myself to feel them, and then labeling them, I became more adept at controlling them. You will, too.

Step 2: Get Curious with (Self-Directed) Compassion

It's not only important to know how you feel; it's also important to know *why* you feel that way. For example, a White person might find themselves feeling highly uncomfortable in conversations about race. That might lead them to shut down and get defensive. They might be tempted to abbreviate the introspective process by just saying to themselves, "I feel uncomfortable." This would be a mistake because without knowing why they're uncomfortable, they won't be able to make the requisite adjustments to engage in these conversations. Remember, emotional discomfort is a sign there's something important going on inside of you. You can't solve a problem if you don't understand it.

Getting curious with compassion also helps make sure we fully understand those emotions we named and acknowledged in step one. Accurately identifying emotions is not as easy as it may sound. For example,
anger is an emotion that is particularly tricky because in many cases it is
not a "primary" emotion, but a *secondary emotion.* "Secondary emotions,"
according to psychology researcher Matthew Tull, "are emotional reactions we have to other emotions."[7] For example, think back to the game of
chess I was playing with Kai. He may have first felt embarrassed because
he made a mistake in the game, and then that feeling of embarrassment
triggered anger.

Because of the psychology of secondary emotions, this process can take
some time. After you label how you're feeling, ask yourself, "What else?"
until *all* of the emotions you're feeling are revealed. Let's go back to the
emotional challenge this book addresses, the nebulous feeling of being
uncomfortable in conversations about race, and dig deeper. Here's how that
internal dialogue could go:

What am I feeling?
I'm feeling uncomfortable.
What else am I feeling?
Well, I'm feeling a little bit scared. I'm afraid of offending someone or
     sounding dumb.
What else?
I'm also feeling a little bit of shame and embarrassment because I feel
     like I *should* know what to do or say. I feel inadequate that I don't.

This is very different from simply saying, "I'm uncomfortable."

Remember, internally-directed Compassionate Curiosity is essentially
a negotiation between different parts of yourself. You're having a conversation with yourself where your goal is a deeper understanding of your own
thoughts and feelings. Sometimes you have to ask multiple questions in different ways to get the information you want. When you ask yourself only one
question, you're likely to get only one, shallow, insufficient response. But if

you stay persistent and curious, you'll often discover that there's more depth to your emotional experience than you initially realized.

After you get a better understanding of *what* you're feeling, it's time to understand *why* you feel that way. This is where you begin to ask yourself "Why?" and keep asking until you get more clarity. Usually, it takes a few "whys" to get to the heart of the matter. Knowing when the analysis has reached its practical conclusion is an imprecise science; however, the simple rule I follow is that if I run out of answers, I stop. Let's go back to the internal dialogue where the person initially said that they feel "uncomfortable" and see how the conversation could progress:

> *What are you feeling?*
> I feel uncomfortable and that discomfort comes from my fear, shame, and embarrassment.
> *Why?*
> Because I care about my BIPOC friends and the world treats them unfairly.
> *Why does that bother me?*
> Because I've been so busy with work and family that I didn't take the time to look around and see some of these problems in society.
> I feel like I should've done better, and learned more, and I'm embarrassed that I didn't. I feel like I let my BIPOC friends down.
> *Why does that bother me?*
> Because I'm a problem solver and it feels like this is a problem I can't solve, so I feel powerless.

By staying curious and digging deeper, you can gain a lot more clarity into your feelings and their source. In this case, the person feels uncomfortable because they feel powerless. So they now know that, when having difficult conversations with others about race, rather than getting overwhelmed by their discomfort to the point where they lash out or shut down, they can steer those conversations in a direction that helps them understand what they can do in each specific situation to be supportive and helpful.

This requires self-compassion. Don't criticize yourself for how you feel or for your desires. For example, you may recognize a discrepancy between your emotional or instinctual response and your stated values. This might be troubling at first, but it gives you an opportunity to reconcile those internal differences and begin to walk in what you deem to be the right direction.

Step 3: Use Joint Problem Solving

In this final stage, we're reconciling differences—in this case, between our heart (our emotions) and mind (our logic and reason). You're asking yourself the following three questions in order to gain clarity about what a potential solution to a problem might look like in the real world:

1. What would satisfy my emotional needs? In other words, what would make me *feel* better?
2. What would satisfy my substantive needs? In other words, what is the actual problem that I need to solve in the real world?
3. What can I do to meet both of those needs at the same time?

To find a solution that meets both your emotional and substantive needs, you need to start off with some level of emotional honesty with yourself. You also need to balance reason and emotion. You can't choose one over the other. You need both to succeed.

The Three Steps in Action

Once you have armed yourself with a deeper understanding of your own feelings and motivations, you can approach the conversation with others in a much more authentic and powerful way. The sooner you can accurately identify and label the emotions that you are feeling, the faster you can get clarity. The faster you can get clarity, the faster you can "tame" those strong feelings and get emotional relief. When you get emotional relief, you can perform at a higher level: you'll think more clearly, make better decisions, and communicate much more effectively, which can lead to significant changes in your perspectives, beliefs, and outcomes.

Let's look at an example of what these three steps, all put together, could look like.

The VP of your department is looking for suggestions for who would be a good leader from your team to step up to the role of manager, and they ask, "What do you think about Julie Chen?" Your initial thought is, "Chen is super smart and an incredibly hard worker, but she doesn't seem like leadership material." But instead of answering immediately, you take five seconds and do a quick internal run-through using the framework:

1. **Acknowledge and validate emotions and beliefs.** *I don't believe Julie Chen would be a good choice. I don't feel comfortable recommending her for this position. I don't feel like she has a strong enough personality to handle the role.*

2. **Get curious with compassion.** *Why do I think she wouldn't be a good choice for leadership? I don't know! I know she does great work. Was it something she said in the past? No, she actually speaks regularly about her leadership aspirations.*

3. **Use joint problem solving (reconciling your emotions and reason).** *I felt like she wouldn't be a good choice, but I don't know why. I genuinely want to treat the people on my team fairly. I don't have any evidence to substantiate my initial gut response. If my initial feelings didn't come from evidence, they likely came from a bias that I didn't know that I had. All of my interactions with her have been positive, she does great work, and she wants to be a leader in the company. I should give her a positive recommendation.*

After going through the process, you tell the VP, "Julie Chen has been one of the best people on my team. I think she's a solid choice."

Rather than simply accepting their initial conclusion that Julie Chen wouldn't be a good choice for leadership, the person in this example slowed down and went through the Compassionate Curiosity framework in order to make sure that they were analyzing the situation appropriately. After pausing and taking a few moments to challenge their own assumptions, they were able to come up with a better, more equitable, answer.

Are You on the Right Train?

While most people probably don't picture actual trains when they think of the term "train of thought," I find it helpful to do just that. I imagine I'm sitting at the train station and have a choice as to whether I'm going to get on any specific train of thought that crosses my mind.

For example, I might, during a difficult conversation, be tempted to think that a person is closed minded, biased, racist, or outright evil. But remembering that whether or not I jump on that train is a choice helps me sit back, almost like a passive observer, and consider which train of thought would be most beneficial for the situation.

In my experience, the first train is often the wrong train. The first train of thought often takes me to a place that's dark and unhelpful. I might need to wait until the third or fourth train before I find a mental state or belief or mindset that is more suitable for the conversation.

In the Compassionate Curiosity framework, acknowledging emotions is identifying the trains as they go by. Getting curious with compassion is asking yourself, "Where is this train of thought headed? Is it true, empowering, and helpful? What other trains could I ride instead?" And then using "joint" problem solving is asking myself which train of thought takes me closest to my desired emotional state and my desired goal.

MORE HELP KEEPING YOUR COOL DURING CONVERSATIONS

As we've discussed, internally directed Compassionate Curiosity is helpful for managing emotions during a conversation; however, there will be times where you need some additional assistance in managing your emotions because, for example, your emotions are too strong to unpack quickly during the flow of the conversation. In those situations, here are three additional tips for keeping your cool:

1. *Use a mantra.* Whenever I find myself starting to get emotional during a conversation, I say "Compassionate Curiosity" to myself. It reminds me of how I should be approaching the conversation to keep it moving in the right direction. This might happen several times during the conversation.

2. *Use box breathing.* Slowing down your breathing helps calm your body's stress response, which in turn allows you to regain cognitive control. To use box breathing, inhale slowly for four seconds, hold for four seconds, exhale slowly for four seconds, and hold for four seconds.

3. *Take notes.* If you have a notepad, you could ask for a few seconds to take notes on what was said; I've found that people are willing to give you up to fifteen to twenty seconds of silence to take notes. Writing has been shown to help process your emotions,[8] because it helps you to "prioritize problems, fears, and concerns" and provides "an opportunity for positive self-talk and identifying negative thoughts and behaviors."[9] And, in the context of difficult conversations, it gives you an opportunity to reset, write out a quick strategy, and regain control of the conversation by asking an insightful, open-ended question. But, to be honest, when I'm emotional, I'm often not even writing anything. I'm just scribbling to feel the pen make contact with the paper. I turn this into a mini-meditation that helps me refocus and regain control.

USING COMPASSIONATE CURIOSITY WITH OTHERS

You've used Compassionate Curiosity to understand your own feelings about a problem, find out what's causing them, and determine the solution you believe best addresses the problem. Now it's time for the external conversation. The same framework allows you to navigate the other person's potential emotional challenges and keep the conversation steered in a productive direction.

Step 1: Acknowledge and Validate the Emotions of Others

In these difficult conversations about race, the number of emotions you may see are vast:

- anger
- sadness
- frustration
- disappointment
- apathy
- confusion
- fear
- disgust

These emotions are normal and understandable, but when the other person is feeling them strongly enough to activate their body's stress response, it's hard to have a constructive conversation. Remember, stress impairs our ability to think rationally. If you aren't able to address the other person's emotional challenges, it's going to be nearly impossible to engage in productive dialogue.

That's why this first step in the framework is the most important part of the process. Before you can address someone's emotional challenges, you have to learn what they are, and accept that they're an important part of the conversation. By encouraging them to name their emotions, then acknowledging and validating them, you help your conversational partner cool their emotional response and bring their rational brain back online.

The methodology here is simple: we're trying to get the other person to label their emotions by saying, "It sounds like," "It seems like," or (if the emotion is clear to see) "I can tell that," then stepping back in order to give them an opportunity to self-reflect. Here are a few examples:

- It sounds like this situation was really frustrating for you.
- It seems like this is really having an impact on you.
- I can tell that this is something you feel strongly about.

They will respond by either confirming or clarifying. Then, you summarize what they said *using the same keywords they used*, and validate their feelings by saying something to the effect of, "I can understand how you feel that way."

Let's say a colleague comes to you, upset. They tell you about a conversation they had where someone made a racially insensitive comment and add that, since joining the company, they've experienced several similar incidents and it's becoming hard to deal with. Instead of denying their experience by saying something like, "I'm sure they didn't mean it that way" or, "It's okay, I'm sure it wasn't that bad," you should first acknowledge their emotions by saying something like, "It sounds like what they said really offended you" or, "I can tell that this situation is having a significant impact on your experience here." This will likely lead them to vent a little bit or share more, in the process labeling more clearly what they're feeling, which will help them begin to lower their level of emotionality.

Next, honor their experience and perspective by letting them know that you understand where they're coming from. You can do this by first giving a brief synopsis of what they said and then validating their emotional experience. For example, you could say, "Okay, so correct me if I'm wrong, but it sounds like the comment they said about [insert a summary of the comment here] was offensive because [insert their rationale here]. Is that correct?" By demonstrating your understanding of what was said and asking for clarification if necessary, it shows that you're listening and that you care enough about what they said to want to get it right.

After they confirm, you finish the validation process by saying something like, "Thanks for clarifying. I can definitely see why what they said made you feel offended." This process does wonders for building trust and managing the emotional temperature of the conversation.

Any time you recognize the presence of an emotion or strongly held belief, acknowledge and validate that emotion before doing anything else. Remember, acknowledgment is not agreement, and validating is not condoning. We might completely disagree with someone, but that doesn't mean we can't still understand what they feel and why. And this acknowledgment and validation is exactly what they need to process their complicated emotions and move toward emotional stability, which will increase the likelihood of the conversation moving in a productive direction.

Addressing emotions before getting into the more substantive part of the conversation is especially important when the person you're talking to is making points that do not align with reality or facts. While there's a difference between facts and feelings, in the heat of the moment they can feel exactly the same. Just because something isn't right doesn't mean that it doesn't *feel* right to them. And just because something isn't true doesn't mean the other person is not emotionally tied to the belief that it is true. This is why, when people are feeling particularly emotional, they often will state opinions or unsubstantiated claims with more certitude than those opinions and claims warrant.

Remember, biases aren't rooted in facts or reality, so trying to combat them with facts or reality alone will often be inefficient at best, and frustratingly futile at worst. If something feels right to the person, your strategy has to address their feelings first, because that is what often underlies a sizable portion of their beliefs.

If my conversation partner states an opinion with emotion, I will address the emotion first, not the point itself. You'll be surprised how many times people's strong positions fade along with their strong emotions. All you need to do is stick to the framework: encourage them to name the emotion, acknowledge it, and validate it. At this stage of the conversation you want to focus *exclusively* on what your partner needs to overcome their emotional hurdle.

If you try to challenge the veracity of their claim directly *before* addressing the emotion behind it, you are likely to run into a frustrating phenomenon known as *psychological entrenchment*—when someone digs in their heels and gets defensive. Many times, by challenging someone's beliefs directly, you are inadvertently making them more committed to their position. This makes your job much harder because they feel forced to repeatedly defend and reinforce it, *making it much harder for them to change their position as the conversation progresses.*[10] The more time they spend vigorously defending themselves, their beliefs, and their opinions, the harder it is for them to adjust those beliefs or opinions without it feeling like a humiliating loss. By then it's no longer about right or wrong for them; it's about winning or losing.

Deepak Malhotra, Harvard professor and author of the books *Negotiating the Impossible* and *Negotiation Genius*, believes that sometimes the best thing you can do for an aggressively stated position is ignore it completely. For example, if someone gives an aggressive ultimatum, Malhotra says, "I don't ask the person to repeat what he said or clarify what he meant. Instead, I pretend he never said it and move on."[11] In our case, in step one of the Compassionate Curiosity framework, instead of attacking or directly challenging the specifics of what was said, we're going to acknowledge and validate the emotions behind it. (Don't worry, there is a time, place, and procedure for strategically challenging the substance of a belief or opinion; just not in step one.)

Especially during this part of the process, you should be listening far more than talking. I like to follow the 70–30 Rule, where I'm listening 70 percent of the time and speaking only 30 percent. This gives the other person space to express their thoughts and emotions. Because we are still in level one communication at this point in the conversation, it's all about understanding their perspective, in order to earn the right to convince them with yours.

Remember, too, that when the other person is in an emotionally reactive state, they aren't ready to be receptive. Trying to convey your message at this stage in the conversation is likely to not only be ineffective but also counterproductive, because the other person may take what you're saying as a threat and respond combatively. Be patient.

Acknowledging these emotions is critical not only because it helps the other person calm their stress response but also because it creates trust and connection. This encourages vulnerability, which allows you to learn more about each other, and lays the foundation you need for collaborative problem solving later in the conversation. If we do not take the time to acknowledge the other person's emotions or, even worse, if we dismiss their emotions, we are communicating that we do not care about them. They may even interpret it as you judging and condemning them for how they feel. Thus, we need to be careful not to reflexively dismiss or contradict what they say about their emotional state.

Most negotiation and communication experts extol the virtues of listening, but I believe that listening, by itself, is overrated; on its own, it's *never* enough. People always say they just want people to listen to them—that they want to be heard—but that's not the full truth. Imagine you're talking to someone and they are on their phone the whole time, never looking up at you or responding in any other way. You'd probably accuse that person of not listening to you. But what if they then repeat back what you said to them verbatim, proving that they were, in fact, listening? Would you feel satisfied? Probably not. But why? They were clearly listening. You were clearly "heard."

The reason is that, although they listened to you, they didn't validate you. They didn't take the time to:

1. show that they cared about you or what you were saying.
2. show that they believe what you are saying, and in particular what you are feeling, is valid.

Although the listener clearly *listened* to what you said, their body language and their verbal response failed to show that they *cared*.

Instead of focusing on listening, I want you to focus on validation, which shows that you care about the other person and respect them. I don't want you to listen from *your* perspective, I want you to listen from *their* perspective. And I want you to take this to the most significant cognitive extreme imaginable. I want you to, as you're listening to them speak, literally envision what it is that they see from their perspective.

What does the room like from their perspective?
When they look at me, what do they see?
What social pressures are they feeling?
How does their lived experience impact how they are perceiving my words?
How do they see me?

Then, as you listen, find opportunities to let them know where you agree with them. Remember in school when your math teacher told you to make sure you showed your work so you could get partial credit, even if you were wrong? Think of yourself as a math teacher; look for the credit you can give. Find some sliver of validity in what they've said. For example, you can validate by simply demonstrating that you can understand how they reached their conclusion based on their perspective.

Finding the validity in what the person I'm talking to is saying isn't always easy; often, it's quite difficult. Let's go back to the task force example from the last chapter, and the company leader who responded with skepticism to assessment results showing it took BIPOC employees, on average, 1.7 years longer to earn a promotion than White peers with the same qualifications. Their argument, "In my experience, if someone is a hardworking go-getter who does their job, then they get a promotion . . . I bet if we were to look into it, all of the people who were promoted in a timely manner deserved it and there was a legitimate reason for holding back the rest."

First, consider why they might be responding that way. Perhaps they were feeling irritated that someone who had worked at the company twenty years fewer than they had was claiming to know more about the company than they did. It also might be the first time they were hearing of any kind of problem, which made them skeptical. If they see themselves as highly perceptive, it might be hard for them to believe they missed such a major problem. And if they believe that the company and its employees are fundamentally just, it would be challenging for them to believe anything but personal work ethic could be at fault.

Then, look for common ground. For example, you might agree with their belief that people should be rewarded for their hard work. You just disagree with whether that's happening in this particular case.

Here's how a response that acknowledges and validates their emotions might then go:

YOU: Correct me if I'm wrong, but it sounds like you're a bit skeptical of the assessment's findings. Is that right?

THEM: Absolutely! I've worked here for thirty years and I've been treated with nothing but respect and I do the same for everyone. I got to where I am today because of hard work and so did everyone else. Everyone here is being treated fairly. I refuse to believe anything different.

Let's pause the conversation here. They are stating their emotions and beliefs using statements that sound like facts. You might be tempted to directly challenge the claim that "everyone here is being treated fairly"—but now is not the time. Why? Because they're not in the right emotional state to adjust their position. They'll dig in their heels, even though you have a robust assessment with data analytics to bolster your point and all they have is their beliefs and personal experience. Remember, when an unsubstantiated fact is stated with emotions, *you address the emotions first, not the veracity of the claim.*

YOU: Okay, I can see where you're coming from. It sounds like based on your experience, you haven't personally seen any instances of unfair treatment. It also sounds like hard work is something that you value and that you believe it should be a key component of whether or not someone gets a promotion. Is that right?

THEM: Exactly! Work ethic and taking personal responsibility for your success are what help people to get ahead. It's not about handouts.

Their emotionality is already starting to calm down a little bit.

YOU: I agree with you. Hard work is extremely important, especially when it comes to promotions. Those are important decisions and they shouldn't be taken lightly.

At this point in the conversation, you'll start to see the signs of releasing tension. Their shoulders may become more relaxed and their facial expression may soften. These are the kinds of signs you want to look for as evidence that the other person's emotional state is shifting.

Since people often tie their self-worth to their positions in these conversations, it can be difficult to adjust their position without feeling as though it's a personal threat to their dignity and self-respect. Validating their perspective assures them you value and respect them, which in turn makes it feel safer and easier for them to adjust their position. You are laying the psychological foundation for them to feel comfortable enough to choose to be open to persuasion.

Once you have lowered the emotional temperature of the room, you can transition to the next step in the process: getting curious with compassion.

Step 2: Get Curious with Compassion

Once you've heard, acknowledged, and validated what they're feeling, it's time for the second step in the Compassionate Curiosity framework: getting curious with compassion, in order to learn, understand, and (if it's part of your goal) begin to persuade.

At this stage of the conversation, your tool of choice is *empathetic inquiry*—questions and statements designed to get the other person to share their perspective. Your goal is to keep them talking. This gives you the chance to (1) deepen your understanding of where they're coming from and (2) begin using the epistemological approach to persuasion, where you ask questions to help them see the potential flaws in their position.

To do this, you want to stick to open-ended questions. However, as much as possible, avoid questions that start with the word *why*. The reason is that *why* questions often are interpreted as judgmental in nature, which in difficult conversations often triggers defensiveness.

Think about when you were a child and your parents or teachers asked you questions that started with *why*, like, "Why did you do that?" or, "Why did you say that?" Those questions usually meant you'd done or said something wrong. That assumption persists into adulthood. When someone asks us a question that starts with *why* in a difficult conversation, we're likely to feel attacked.

To avoid this, stick with *who*, *what*, *where*, *when*, and *how* questions. If you want to ask a question that starts with *why*, try to rephrase it as a question that starts with *what* or *how*.[12] For example, instead of, "Why do you think the assessment is flawed?" ask, "What are your concerns about the assessment?"

You want to approach this part of the conversation in a way that's designed to diminish the other person's attachment to their position, not strengthen it. With the first question, the person's response will likely take the form of *defending* their position; with the second question, the person's response will likely take the form of *sharing* their perspective. You gather the same information without the same risk of entrenchment.

Sometimes, depending on the level of tension in the conversation, asking *any* question may still feel too aggressive. Remember, your goal is to make people feel safe, so they are comfortable answering your questions and sharing information, especially when it's sensitive in nature. Curiosity expert Becki Saltzman suggests an incredibly simple tweak to help take the sting out of challenging or potentially threatening questions: add the phrase "Out of curiosity" before a question to soften its impact.[13] Other handy sentence softeners for getting someone to share more information include:

- Tell me more about . . .
- Help me to understand . . .

To get someone to expound on a point, you can also use a tool called *mirroring*, which Chris Voss, FBI hostage negotiator and author of *Never Split the Difference*, calls "the closest thing to a Jedi mind trick that you have."[14] With mirroring, all you do is repeat the last one to three words of what the other person says with an upward intonation. This leads them to delve deeper into their prior point. For example:

"We don't need to create any affinity groups in our company because all they do is cause problems."

"Cause problems?"

"Yeah, they seem to cause needless division in companies and force people to draw racial lines that I think could be ultimately hurtful. I don't know if it's worth the risk. It just doesn't make sense to me."

Mirroring is a basic but powerful way to get more information and even gently challenge the previous assertion without sounding combative.

Knowing what questions to ask when can be a daunting task. To manage this, I like to use the funnel technique, in which you start the conversation by asking broader questions, then get more specific as the conversation progresses and you get more information. For example, when conducting a mediation, I would always start by speaking to the parties individually (following the rule of smaller conversations I mentioned in the last chapter). I would begin these conversations with statements like, "Tell me how we got to this point" or broad, open-ended questions like, "What are you looking to get out of this mediation?"

In other words, I would start the conversation as if I knew nothing, even though I always reviewed the case files thoroughly beforehand. I never want to assume that I already know what each of the participants wants, why they want it, or even the facts of the case.

This helps for a number of reasons. First, I'm often surprised at what *really* matters to the parties. For example, I was mediating a case between warring neighbors. They shared a driveway and they were suing each other because they couldn't agree on how to coexist in such close proximity. As one of the participants was talking, they complained about the neighbors' dog more than three times. That made me curious. I adjusted my strategy and asked more questions about the issue with the dog. It turned out that, after hours of mediation, the only way we were able to break through and solve the problem was by incorporating the dog issue into the agreement.

Second, reading the facts in a case file is very different from hearing a person tell the story themselves. As you listen to what they say, pay attention to these three things:

1. *Pace and volume.* If they shift their rate of speech or volume up or down while talking about a specific topic.
2. *Repetition.* If they repeat the same thing multiple times during the conversation.
3. *Body Language.* If there are consistent shifts in body language while they are discussing a particular point. For example, if they cross their arms and lean back every time they talk about a specific person.

These are all clues that you've hit upon something that would benefit from further investigation. Whatever they are talking about when they exhibit these signals is where you should focus your questions and dig deeper, because it's likely that there is something important beneath the surface.

My typical conversational pattern, both in difficult conversations about race and when I'm building relationships in general, is as follows:

- ask.
- listen.
- summarize.

I repeat this pattern in some fashion throughout the entire conversation. Also, whenever possible, I ask the question that restarts this pattern immediately after the summary. This helps ensure that I can guide the conversation in productive directions.

As you cycle through asking, listening, and summarizing, the gaps in your knowledge will fill, and you may start running out of questions to ask. Once I reach that point, I like to ask a question that helps cover any questions I would have benefited from asking, but didn't. For example:

- What else do you think I should know?
- What am I missing?
- What other concerns are top of mind for you?

In some regards, Compassionate Curiosity can feel like an indirect route to persuasion. However, direct challenges often encourage direct opposition. The Compassionate Curiosity approach increases your likelihood of success because it inspires less resistance.

Avoid the Word *But*

Many people make the mistake of using the word *but* when summarizing and responding to what another person shares. They may say something like, "I understand that you feel frustrated, *but* . . ." This is problematic because, when you say *but*, it negates whatever is said before it. If you begin by acknowledging the other person's emotion, then use the word *but*, you immediately *in*validate, rather than validate, that emotion. They'll take it as you saying that your perspective on their emotion is more important than theirs. This often *increases* the emotionality in the conversation instead of *decreasing* it, because when you put your feelings above someone else's, they often feel the subconscious need to escalate.

Fortunately, there is a simple solution. Replace the word *but* with the phrase *the problem is* . . . Then fill in the blank with the problem you see in the previous statement. For example, instead of saying, "I understand that you disagree with the findings of the assessment, *but* your lived experience is different from that of our BIPOC colleagues," you could say something more like, "I understand that you disagree with the findings of the assessment. *The problem is* that your lived experience is different from that of our BIPOC colleagues." This lets you acknowledge the other person's position respectfully while clearly articulating how your perspective differs from theirs. You don't want to risk them feeling as though you were disrespecting them by not listening or giving reasonable consideration to their perspective. If they feel disrespected or that you haven't meaningfully considered what they said, they are likely to get stuck on the point because they don't think you get it. By contrast, this approach allows you to show that even though you get where they're coming from, you still see it differently, which allows you to share your perspective with less resistance.

Oftentimes, the issue I see is that the other person is overlooking something important, in which case I use *The problem is* to bring it to their attention. Then finish my statement by asking another open-ended question that is designed to get them to consider what I believe they're currently overlooking. For example, "It sounds like you're reluctant to implement this new program because of the timing. And that makes sense—it would be challenging. The problem is that when you look at the rest of the year, this is the only window available to put it into action. Considering that, what do you think it would take for us to make this work?" This question gets the person to recognize time constraints they may not have been considering. It also triggers creative problem solving by getting them to focus on what would need to change in order to realistically bring the program to life within those time constraints.

Striking the Right Tone

The first time my older son, Kai, held Dominic, his little brother, Dominic was three days old. As newborns often do, Dominic started to cry. Upon seeing his little brother in tears, Kai started to cry, too. Why? It's the same reason why yawning is oddly contagious—mirror neurons.[15]

Mirror neurons are brain cells that are activated whenever we observe others' behavior.[16] They play a role in empathy, and are why, when we see someone smile or yawn, we often do the same. As neuroscientists J. A. C. J. Bastiaansen, Marc Thioux, and Christian Keysers explain, "seeing the emotions of others . . . recruits regions involved in experiencing similar emotions."[17] Emotions are contagious; the emotional states of others have an impact on our own.

This is why we want to be especially mindful of our tone in difficult conversations. If we seem apprehensive, tense, hostile, or aggressive, the other person in the conversation can "catch" the same emotional state. This can create a problematic emotional feedback loop, and these conversations are already emotional enough.

The good news is that a positive tone has the same effect. In some of my trainings, I have people break into pairs to play a game. I instruct them to look into each other's eyes as one of them puts on a big smile and the other tries to keep a straight face. In most of these pairs, both people inevitably end up smiling and laughing. Why? The smile triggers the mirror neurons of the straight-faced partner, overpowering their neutrality by eliciting positive emotions.

What emotional contagion suggests is that if you're uncomfortable talking about race, other people are more likely to feel uncomfortable talking about it with you. Conversely, you can make people feel more comfortable talking to you just by showing that *you* are comfortable in the conversation and avoiding inadvertently triggering sentiments of negativity in your body language, tone, or word choice.

Remember what we said in the last chapter: *when you lose your cool in a difficult conversation, you give the other person an excuse to stop listening.*

Have you ever been accused of yelling when you didn't think that you were? I find that when I'm emotional, I typically speak much louder and much faster than I realize. My performance in difficult conversations improved exponentially when I started to use this simple technique: low and slow. When I'm feeling emotional, I focus on lowering my voice and slowing my speech. This makes it less likely that I will be perceived as being mean or aggressive or that I will make a mistake, and it makes my words more impactful because I minimize the likelihood of emotional distractions. In other words, my conversation partner can focus on what I'm saying more than on how I'm saying it. It's a minor adjustment that can make a huge impact.

This Is Not Tone Policing

Before we move on to the third part of the framework, I want to add a quick note about *tone policing.* Tone policing is focusing on how a person says something when they're experiencing emotional distress, rather than on what the speaker is saying.

For example, a BIPOC colleague of mine once accidentally discovered that she made $30,000 less than her White counterpart who was on the same level. This was infuriating to her, especially considering the fact that she had been there longer, had more career experience, and, according to her manager, consistently performed better in their quarterly reviews. When she brought this to the attention of her superiors, instead of responding with empathy or providing an explanation, they commented that they didn't like how she was speaking to them.

Tone policing is often used against BIPOC individuals when they discuss racial issues in the workplace. Because these individuals can carry a lot of painful emotional baggage associated with race, that emotion may manifest in the conversation. Their claims are often disregarded not because they are illegitimate but because the ways they expressed those claims are deemed inappropriate or make others feel uncomfortable. In my friend's situation, her superiors, rather than seeing her as a colleague who was treated unfairly, labeled her as an "angry Black woman" and used that as an excuse to disregard her legitimate claim of injustice.

I want to be very clear that, when I talk about the importance of tone in a conversation, I do not mean for you to police *other people's* tones. Doing so is not only cruel; it is also ineffective, because it typically *increases* their emotional volatility while eroding the fabric of the relationship. However, I do suggest that you consider making the strategic choice to be mindful of your own tone during these conversations, because the wrong tone or approach can have a detrimental impact on your message regardless of its content. Is it fair? No. Is it real? Yes. Again, this is a personal strategic choice that only you can make.

What is an "appropriate" tone is context dependent. For example, when I'm talking to my Guyanese mother, I am a lot more expressive when I'm upset because, in Caribbean culture, emotional conversations can be a little bit more, dare I say, *spicy*. When I'm negotiating in the business world or serving as a mediator, I am much more reserved. When communicating with Whitney, my wife, I found that the approach I use with my mother was too hot and the approach to use as a lawyer was too cold, so I had to find what I call the "Goldilocks Zone" that blends expressiveness with restraint and empathy.

This is an example of the authentic code switching we talked about in chapter four. Each context and each relationship has its own "culture," and I need to match my tone to what is considered culturally appropriate for each space. As you start to pay attention to this, you'll start to get an idea of what works and what doesn't work in your workplace, and with different individuals there. Each interaction you have can give you valuable feedback on the "appropriate tone" for similar future interactions.

It's Possible to Be Too Curious

A word of caution, especially for White folks, regarding curiosity: it's not always easy for BIPOC to share their feelings or their perspectives on racial issues. Your desire to understand may inadvertently put pressure on other people to relive racial trauma. So as well-intentioned as you may be in your desire to learn, you must remember that it's not someone else's responsibility to educate you on race-related issues in society. Take responsibility for your own education by using books and the internet to learn on your own as much as possible—and pay attention to subtle signs of discomfort to see when you may be pushing too far.

Step 3: Use Joint Problem Solving

The final step of the Compassionate Curiosity framework is collaborative problem solving. We've worked through the emotional challenges, we've gathered information, and now we're asking the question: How can we work together to create a better future?

It's important to make sure that the other person feels as though they are playing a role in the decision-making process. This is because collaboration builds commitment. The more they contribute to the conversation and the solution, the more likely they are to stay engaged, not just for the duration of the conversation, but afterwards, when they are making any necessary changes. In other words, their participation creates *buy-in*, the "acceptance of and willingness to actively support and participate in something."[18]

I think of this step in the process as a brainstorming session where both parties share ideas and potential solutions. I usually start by describing my proposal for how to solve the problem, structuring it in the following way:

1. Given what we know now, I believe that [*describe idea here*] would be beneficial for everyone because [*explain why it works for both you and them, ideally using their own words regarding their goals*].
2. What are your thoughts?

Then I listen, to hear their perspective, and we repeat the process until we reach a decision or get some clarity as to what we plan to do going forward.

Sometimes the other person might be lacking in creativity or hesitant to engage in a brainstorming session with you. If that is the case, you can try using what I call the "magic question": *If you could wave a magic wand and solve this problem, what would the solution look like? What would you make happen?* This helps them to think outside of the box by expanding their view of what is possible.

If their hesitation comes from trepidation or fear, I find it helpful to approach brainstorming in the form of a hypothetical question. I pinpoint the emotion that is causing their hesitation and then say something like, *You mentioned earlier that saying something publicly about what's been happening related to race is scary for you as the leader of this company. The problem is that you've also recognized that, based on what you've observed, you don't believe that staying silent on this issue is viable, either. Hypothetically, if you knew that after you made a public statement, the business would continue to function in more or less the same way as before, what would you say?*

People are frequently uncomfortable wrestling with reality, but more comfortable wrestling with fiction. So, create a safer hypothetical world for them to problem solve in. Once they can break through the initial barrier and start to visualize what a solution might look like in their fictional world, they are more likely to be able to see viable solutions in the real world.

The Power of Positive Reinforcement

Throughout the conversation, you want to reinforce the behavior you want from the other person by letting them know explicitly that you appreciate the good things that they do. This increases the likelihood that they will continue to do those things, and makes the conversation flow with less friction.

For example, when I used to conduct mediations, I wanted people to share information and trust me. To encourage this, throughout the conversation I would say things like:

- "I appreciate your candor."
- "I appreciate you explaining that thoroughly to me."
- "I know that you are in a difficult position right now and I appreciate how you are handling yourself in this conversation. Most people wouldn't be able to respond in this way."
- "Thank you for that. You're making this conversation easier."

What I am doing here is making it clear that their efforts are recognized and appreciated. I am creating a positive persona for them, and implicitly conveying that I expect them to continue to comport themselves in this way. According to Harvard negotiation experts Roger Fisher and Dan Shapiro, people have a fundamental need to feel appreciated, which is the desire to be understood and valued.[19] When people feel more appreciated during a difficult conversation, they are more likely to communicate cooperatively. In my experience, the easiest way to do this is to simply say, "I appreciate [insert something they said or did]." Even when one party in a mediation is being particularly mean or nasty, I try to find *something* to appreciate about their behavior. Once I do this, their behavior almost always begins to improve.

What If the Other Person Gets Stuck?

There are two questions I'm often asked regarding the Compassionate Curiosity framework:

- What if the person is stuck in the negative emotional state, and no matter how much you acknowledge the emotion, it doesn't go away?
- How can you tell whether somebody is stuck emotionally versus intentionally being obstinate and using emotion as a tactic to prevent progress?

In truth, it doesn't matter whether the other person is preventing the conversation from moving forward intentionally or unintentionally, because the outcome is the same: their extended period of emotionality is hindering the productivity of the conversation. This is an example of where it's important to assume positive intent. If you assume that the other person is trying to intentionally derail the conversation, you are going to lose patience quickly. Your ever-increasing negative emotions will drain your willpower and emotional restraint, making you less effective.

You can only devote so much time to acknowledging the other person's emotions before it becomes clear that your efforts are futile—that they aren't able or willing to move on to solving the problem. If they won't budge from their position, you may have only two choices: (1) ending the conversation and resuming at another time—when, hopefully, they'll be more receptive—or, if you don't have the luxury of waiting, (2) advancing the conversation despite the persistent emotionality.

It helps to set expectations at the beginning of the conversation as to its length. Let the other person know how much time you have and why. When doing this, you want to attribute the time limit to something external, so they don't feel as though you don't think they're important enough to warrant more time. For example, "Unfortunately, my next meeting starts in forty-five minutes. So I might need to move the conversation along at some points in order to make sure that we address what's most important to you. I want you to know that the only reason I'm doing that is because I want to make sure I can hear your perspective. Your voice matters." That allows you to set a loose timeline for the conversation, while also reassuring them that you find what they have to say valuable.

Then, during the conversation:

- *Stay aware of your time limit.* Enter conversations with a shot clock in your mind. For example, if you only have forty-five minutes, you could assign a mental time limit of thirty minutes for acknowledging and validating emotions and getting curious with compassion before moving the conversation into joint problem solving.

- *Be on guard for signals of slowing conversational advancement.* A major sign that the conversation is stalling is when the other person is repeating facts and rehashing the same feelings.
- *If needed, summarize and push the conversation forward.* For example, "Correct me if I'm wrong, but it sounds like you're saying [insert summary]. Is that right?" After they confirm your understanding, you can say something like, "We're running low on time. Is there anything that you *haven't* told me yet that I should know?" This signals to them that the conversation needs to continue to progress, and lets you respectfully move it along.

Don't Get Stuck in the Past

Although racial trauma, transgressions, and offenses live in the past, they profoundly influence the present and the future. The more that you dwell on the past in these conversations, the more likely it is that the conversation will tip toward negativity. That's why, with Compassionate Curiosity, we utilize what's called *future-focused problem solving.* We want to acknowledge emotions and the past just enough that people feel seen, heard, understood, and appreciated. Then, as much as possible, we want to direct their attention to the future because, when it comes down to it, the reason we have difficult conversations is to create a better future together.

The challenge here is that, even though you want your conversation partner to be focused on the future, they may find it difficult to stop dwelling on the past. The way you move the conversation forward in these moments is by treating their focus on the past the same way you would an emotional response: you acknowledge it and you validate it. You summarize it to demonstrate that you understand. Then you shift the conversation by asking an open-ended question that is focused on the future.

Here's an example of a conversation you might have with a colleague who is offended because they were publicly accused of being racist online:

THEM: They called me a racist! I've never been more offended in my life. It's absolutely preposterous. Instead of going to social media and committing a public character assassination, how about you come talk to me as a person? How does that sound? This situation is absolutely ridiculous.

YOU: It sounds like what they posted about you really offended you and you're frustrated with how things are going. Is that a fair assessment? [*Acknowledging the emotion*]

THEM: Hell yeah! To be honest, I'm really pissed off about this.

YOU: That makes sense. I can understand why you're pissed off about it. I'm sure it didn't feel good to see people say that about you. [*Validating the emotion*]

THEM: Yeah, this really is the low point for my career. (Voice softening) I'm just not sure what to do next.

YOU: Best-case scenario, what would you like to happen out of this? [*Getting curious with compassion*]

THEM: I need people to know that I'm not a racist. I have a great reputation in the community . . . or I did, at least. Now I don't know what people think about me and that bothers me. I just want people to know that I'm not an asshole. I don't have a racist bone in my body.

YOU: Are you willing to take an X-ray to prove it?*

(Both laugh.)

YOU: Okay, but on a more serious note: it sounds like your primary goal is protecting your reputation and making sure that people know who you *really* are. Am I understanding that right? [*Acknowledging the emotion*]

THEM: That's exactly right.

---

* *Note*: This is a little "Kwame-ism" here. I love injecting humor in these conversations to lighten the mood, but you need a decent relationship with the person for this to work. Otherwise, it could seem as though you are making light of the situation, so use humor in difficult conversations with caution.

YOU: Okay, considering what was said about you, I think one of the worst strategic missteps you could make right now is coming out forcefully and saying, "I'm not a racist." I think people might scoff and say, "That's exactly what a racist would say!" So it can't just be about what you say; it also needs to be about what you do. If you give that predictable response, you might make things worse. [*Using joint problem solving*]

THEM: So what do I do, just roll over and give up? Do I let people attack me and destroy my reputation?

YOU: No, not at all. We have to address what was said. While we might not agree with how they went about it, I think we need to take a hard look at their concerns and see what changes need to be made.

THEM: Listen, I'm definitely open to that. I know I'm not perfect and I know my company isn't perfect, either.

YOU: That's good to hear. I think we should get the rest of the leadership together to review what was said and consider its merits. Then, I think we should reach out to the staff and survey them to get an idea of their perspective. After we gather that information, we'll be able to make a more well-reasoned decision and carry out the appropriate changes. But time is of the essence. The longer we wait, the worse this will get.

In this example, we can see that the person was initially focusing on the past—on what had happened and how it made them feel. The only way to move them past that fixation was by acknowledging their perspective and their emotions, then reorienting the conversation in a more productive direction by focusing on the future.

Pulling It All Together

A friend of mine discovered, after running the numbers, that when their company brought in contractors to manage IT and legal projects, professional development training, and other kinds of work, they used White-owned businesses 96 percent of the time. This initially infuriated them, but then they realized it provided them with an opportunity to raise awareness of the problem and do something about it. They were in the C-suite, so they knew they were uniquely positioned to make a difference.

They talked to the company president about the problem and asked if they could put it on the agenda for the monthly executive meeting. The president said no because there were already too many things on the agenda.

"What about next month?" my friend asked.

The president said, "We'll see."

Before the meeting the following month, the same thing happened— my friend brought it up and the president said that there wasn't enough time to discuss it. That's when my friend realized that if they were not more assertive, this important topic might never be seriously considered. They weren't sure whether the president was dodging the discussion intentionally, but regardless of intent, it was clear my friend needed to take more initiative if the situation was going to improve.

So, they decided to have a conversation with the president one on one, using the situation + impact + invitation framework to kick things off.

My friend began, "Like I mentioned last month, I did some research and found out that 96 percent of our outsourced contracts go to White-owned businesses. I believe that we're missing out on an opportunity to support BIPOC businesses in our community, and I want to see if you'd be open to having a quick conversation with me about it."

The president agreed and my friend followed up by framing the conversation with: "I really admire how engaged and involved you've been in our recent inclusion efforts at the company. I wanted to bring this up to you because I know you—probably more so than anybody else in the C-suite— want to make sure that our company is doing everything you can to be more equitable. I'd love to hear your thoughts on the situation."

The president was quiet for a moment and said, "Listen, I appreciate what you said, but we've been using a lot of those contractors for years. I don't think it's right to take contracts away from them just because of their skin color."

My friend immediately wanted to jump in and correct the implication that they wanted to take away contracts because of skin color, but recognized this as a potential detour in the conversation. Despite thinking it was an unfair characterization and feeling a little bit defensive, they stuck to the framework. They recognized that there was emotion at play, and acknowledged and validated it.

MY FRIEND: "Okay, so it sounds like you want to make sure that the contractors we have are being treated fairly and that they don't lose the contracts that they have because of their skin color, is that right?"

THE COMPANY PRESIDENT: "Exactly."

MY FRIEND: "That makes sense, and I agree with you—I think that would be unfair. I don't think anybody should lose their current contract. And you said that we've been using some of those contractors for a long time, so it sounds like you have a pretty good relationship with a few of them, is that right?"

THE COMPANY PRESIDENT: "Yeah. We have great relationships, and the majority of our contractors do incredible work."

MY FRIEND: "Absolutely—relationships matter in business, so I'm on the same page with you there."

At this point, my friend noticed that the president was a lot more relaxed than he had been at the beginning of the conversation. So they transitioned into the second step of the framework: getting curious with compassion.

MY FRIEND: "Like I said, I understand that you don't want people to lose their contracts. Let's just focus on that number, though: 96 percent of our contracts are going to White companies. What kind of message do you think that sends to the BIPOC who work here?"

THE COMPANY PRESIDENT: (thinks silently for a moment) "That's a good question. I guess I never thought of that. I really don't know; I mean, I guess it probably doesn't feel very good."

My friend took the silence as a sign that the company president was more open to suggestions than he was earlier on in the conversation and decided to transition into step three, using joint problem solving.

MY FRIEND: (laughs) "Yeah, I think that's probably a fair assessment. What do you think it would take for us to start to change that number while still treating our previous contractors with the respect that they deserve?"

THE COMPANY PRESIDENT: "I think one thing we could do is revise our request-for-proposal procedure."

MY FRIEND: "Revise the procedure?" [*Mirroring*]

THE COMPANY PRESIDENT: "Yeah, if we're at 96 percent of our business going to White-owned companies, it makes me think that minority-owned businesses aren't applying at the same rate, and I wonder why."

MY FRIEND: "That's a great question. I'm not sure. It's definitely something that I could look into. What else do you think we could do?"

THE COMPANY PRESIDENT: "I don't know. Our process is pretty simple. We just put out the request for proposals, look at the responses, and then consider the skills and the cost and choose who we think is best."

MY FRIEND: "Okay. What do you think about sending some folks from our team out to minority business expos? That might put us right in front of more minority businesses to let them know who we are and how they could help."

THE COMPANY PRESIDENT: "I think that's a great idea, and I think there'll be a few people on our team that would really enjoy getting the opportunity to do things like that."

MY FRIEND: "Great, what are our next steps?"

THE COMPANY PRESIDENT: "Well, I'd like you to do some more research on our request-for-proposal procedure to see what that looks like and then talk with the DEI committee to see what we could do to make that change. Also, see if anybody would be interested in going with us to those expos. It would probably be helpful to get more ideas involved other than just ours, so let's put this on the agenda for the next meeting to get more people in the conversation."

MY FRIEND: "That sounds great."

While it's easy to get overwhelmed, this conversation shows us that even though these conversations are emotional and can be complex, our approach can—and should—stay simple. Remember, you don't get style points for how you have a conversation. As long as you stick to the framework, you'll know what to say, when to say it, and how to say it for maximum impact.

The framework is fluid. For example, if the other person is not experiencing an emotional barrier, this lets you start off instead with getting curious with compassion. Then, after you gather more information and start brainstorming solutions, you might recognize that they're getting emotional and need to acknowledge and validate their emotions at that point.

Your task is to take this framework and make it your own. If you become rigid and dogmatic with the approach, you will struggle. It needs to be organic, it needs to flow, and it needs to feel authentic.

The Compassionate Curiosity framework is rooted in the philosophy that the key to persuasion is to spend more time listening than talking. This takes pressure off of you because your goal is more to learn than it is to teach. It makes the problem of not knowing what to say less of a concern.

What's fascinating about the Compassionate Curiosity framework is that, although you are speaking less, you are exercising more control over the conversation, which in turn gives you a greater likelihood of success. But success isn't just about doing the right things; it's also about not doing the wrong things. The next chapter points out some common mistakes that can affect how you perform in these difficult conversations so that you can keep things moving in a productive direction.

DISCUSSION QUESTIONS

- Think of a difficult conversation about race that you need to have. What are the three emotions that best describe how you are feeling now or may potentially feel during the conversation?
- How will you use the Compassionate Curiosity framework *internally* to manage those emotions?
- What are the top three emotions that the other person is likely to experience during the conversation? Why might they feel that way?
- What will you say to acknowledge each of those emotions and validate them by letting the other person know that it makes sense to you that they feel that way?
- What are three open-ended questions that you could ask during the conversation to help you get a better sense of their perspective?

CHAPTER
SIX

AVOID COMMON MISTAKES

Even armed with the tools and strategies you've learned so far, you are bound to make mistakes when having difficult conversations about race, especially at the beginning. You are trying to change long-term patterns of thinking while learning new techniques. You can't expect to be an expert right out of the gate. You also may not be practiced in talking about race generally, and the discomfort these conversations elicit can cause stress.

That's okay. Embrace that feeling of discomfort and wear it as a badge of honor; it is a signal that you are on the right track. Discomfort means you are growing, learning something new, and expanding your comfort zone. Know that you are doing the best job you can at your current position of understanding, and try not to ruminate over conversational mistakes you made in the past or be so afraid of making new ones that you stop having these important conversations. Remember, not having the conversation at all is almost always the biggest mistake you can make.

Still, by learning what some of the most common mistakes are, you'll be less likely to make them, and you'll know how to react if you do. The seven examples of mistakes in this chapter aim to help you move forward with more confidence and hopefully give you some direction when you fall short.

MISTAKE #1: SPEAKING DIFFERENT LANGUAGES

Just because we're both speaking English doesn't mean that we're speaking the same language. At this point in history, the world is changing so rapidly that our language is struggling to keep up. The same word can mean different things to different people. And some of the terms you use may be completely foreign to your conversation partner. Think, for example, about the use and connotations of personal pronouns in the last few years. The first time someone asked me for my "PGPs," I first had to ask what PGP stood for. (For those of you who are about to google "PGP," it stands for *preferred gender pronouns*.)

When someone uses a word you don't understand, or you use a word you think the other person might not understand, your safest bet is to stop the conversation and get or provide clarification. While asking for a definition sounds like an incredibly basic principle, it is not. Some people would rather misunderstand a term than be embarrassed by displaying a gap in their knowledge. They are afraid of being vulnerable enough to admit they don't understand. And if either of you is unclear on what the other person is actually saying, both of you will struggle to communicate effectively.

Defining terms also helps avoid *semantic arguments*, which focus on disagreement over the definition of the words being used rather than the relevant facts. Consider affirmative action, a topic that has sparked passionate debate for years. According to the Legal Information Institute at Cornell Law School, *affirmative action* is defined as "a set of procedures designed to eliminate unlawful discrimination among applicants, remedy the results of such prior discrimination, and prevent such discrimination in the future."[1] But what's interesting is that both the people who are for affirmative action and those who are against it often rest the basis of their argument on the concept of *fairness*. What does it mean for something to be "fair"? People arguing for affirmative action usually define fair as disadvantaged populations receiving additional support to compensate for structural inequities and years of discrimination. People arguing against affirmative action define fair as treating everyone exactly the same regardless of their background or circumstances. Using the word *fairness* in a conversation about affirmative action is therefore challenging and largely ineffective because both parties see the term differently.

Semantic arguments are a seductive distraction when having a difficult conversation. They seem germane at the time, but they are actually a detour on the conversational highway because, in many cases, simply changing the words that you use could circumvent needless resistance by conveying meaning in a way that both parties can understand and respect.

Here's an example of a conversation I had with a friend that shows this in action.

THEM: I've been attacked by people telling me to check my privilege. It's like they're trying to make me feel bad about my accomplishments just because I'm a White guy. My family was poor and I had to work hard to get where I am.

ME: It sounds like the word *privilege* really got to you.

THEM: Yeah, man. It's divisive and insulting.

ME: I see where you're coming from. I know you and I know you worked hard. I can understand why you feel insulted. What was the context?

THEM: We were talking about racism in America, and I said I believe racism is real and it still has an impact today. But at the same time, I believe this is the best country in the world and if we work hard, we can overcome poverty. Then I shared my story and my coworker dropped the "check your privilege" line on me. I didn't have any privilege! We were on food stamps my whole life.

ME: What does privilege mean to you?

THEM: It means things are easier for me because I'm White. Isn't that it?

ME: Not quite. I can't speak to what was in their heads when they used that term, but often when someone uses the word *privilege*, what they mean is relative advantage. Some advantages are earned, some advantages are unearned, and some are a mix of both.

THEM: Kwame, that's what I'm saying! I didn't have any advantages.

ME: Let me ask you a question. If you and I go to a basketball court and they are picking teams and they have to pick between you and me, who are they going to pick?

THEM: Okay, you're picking on the short guy. They'd pick you because you're taller than me and . . .

ME: And?

THEM: Because you're Black?

ME: Right. Without seeing us play they'd probably have that assumption. Those are two unearned privileges I have over you in that situation.

THEM: Okay, that makes sense.

ME: Here's another one. I'm Black and my wife is Black, but growing up I had a more privileged life. She grew up in the inner city with a single mom, and from time to time they didn't have a place to stay. My parents immigrated to the US to continue their education. My dad is a surgeon and my mom has a PhD and is a professor. That gave me more resources, which meant I avoided some of the chronic life stressors that Whitney had to endure. The privilege of more resources was unearned by me. Then I went to college and graduated with three degrees. That privilege of education is both earned and unearned because even though I worked hard, I had the privileges of, for example, growing up in a safe community, being able to focus on education, sports, and extracurriculars during high school and college instead of having to work, and I consistently had access to health care, all because of my parents' financial support.

THEM: All that makes sense, but how do I have *White* privilege?

ME: Have you ever been discriminated against based on your name alone?

THEM: No.

ME: When you are looking for children's books for your kids, do you struggle to find main characters who look like them?

THEM: No.

ME: How hard is it to surround yourself with people who look like you in a professional setting?

THEM: Not hard at all.

ME: Let's end with a fun one: How hard is it for you to find a "flesh"-colored Band-Aid?

(Both laugh.)

THEM: Okay this is making more sense now. It's not really a personal attack against me, it's more a recognition that, regardless of whether I wanted it or not, there are some benefits of being White in America that are kind of invisible. Is that it?

ME: Exactly.

The dictionary definition of a word isn't important. What's important is what the person you're talking to believes the word to mean. Let's say you're having a conversation about inclusion in the workplace. Do you know what inclusion means to the person you are speaking with? If the answer is no, that might be both the source of their resistance and what's really causing the breakdown in your conversation. Clarifying your respective definitions might be enough to steer the conversation back in a productive direction.

You and your partner may not always be able to reconcile the various terms being used. When this happens to me, I increase my precision of language by using the definition of the word *as I'm using it in this specific context* while omitting the term itself.

Let's say you're the head of DEI for your organization and you're talking to company leaders about increasing diversity and addressing issues of inclusion. According to the US Census, 60.1 percent of Americans iden-tify as "White alone, not Hispanic or Latino" whereas the other 39.9 per-cent identify as BIPOC.[2] However, in your organization, only 8.6 percent of employees are BIPOC. After you tell them, "Right now, it's hard for our BIPOC colleagues to not look around and feel like they're token minorities," the leader of human resources shocks you by responding with frustration. They say, "That's not fair at all. We've been exceptionally respectful of the talent and skills of our BIPOC colleagues! It's not fair to insinuate that we're not trying to address our diversity issue."

The problem here is that, while you are using the term *token employee* to describe a situation where BIPOC see so few colleagues like them-selves that the absence is conspicuous to them, the HR head understands tokenism as an institutional practice where companies reluctantly hire just enough BIPOC candidates to avoid lawsuits regardless of their qualifica-tions. And, since they are in charge of human resources, they took that as a direct attack on their morality and credibility.

You won't always know when you and your conversation partner are using different definitions of a term. Sometimes, though, their language will clue you in. Responses like, "That's an unfair mischaracterization," "What are you insinuating?" or, "How could you think I would _____?" are all indications that you might be dealing with a semantic issue. Now is not the time to defend yourself; instead, focus on them. You need more information—so ask them for it!

For example, if you find yourself in a semantic argument that centers on the word *injustice*, you could say something like, "I'm going to be honest with you. I'm not entirely sure what you mean when you use the word *injus-tice* in this context. Can you help me understand what you mean when you use that term?" Confessing that you're confused, and using the softening phrases we learned last chapter like "Out of curiosity" or "Can you help me to understand" to sound less aggressive, can help you pinpoint the dis-connect in a manner that decreases the likelihood that they can interpret anything you say as hostile.

Then, once you've identified the source of the breakdown in communication, ask for the chance to clarify what you meant. In the tokenism example I offered, for instance, you might clarify: "What I'm saying is that, as the DEI lead for the company, I've noticed that our inclusion scores are suffering in large part due to the lack of diversity. Our numbers are simply too low. If we're not able to address this in a meaningful way, it's going to make our retention issue even worse."

In general, the more specific you are about what you mean, the less likely it is that the other person will misunderstand you, and the more likely it is that the conversation will be constructive. Sometimes, when we use broad terminology in describing a problem, it makes it more difficult to understand the problem and create meaningful solutions. For example, in 2020 and 2021, hate crimes against Asian Americans rose dramatically. According to the Center for the Study of Hate and Extremism, anti-Asian hate crimes rose 145 percent in 2020. Overall, however, the number of hate crimes dropped 6 percent.[3] In this case, saying that "BIPOC" have experienced an increase in hate crimes would be inaccurate, as well as unhelpful for determining a course of action. To address this specific issue, we need to pay special attention to Asian Americans, because they're the ones being affected. The clearer our language is, the easier it is to communicate with each other and to determine effective solutions.

MISTAKE #2: RELYING ON EGOCENTRIC PERSUASION VERSUS EMPATHETIC PERSUASION

Egocentric persuasion is when someone assumes that what they find to be persuasive will also be persuasive to other people. It would be wonderful if this were true—if there was a one-size-fits-all solution that would let you convince someone else to agree with you, every time—but we know better. The individuality of people's histories, biases, self-interests, and personal incentives means there is no single method of persuasion or problem-solving technique that will work in every case.

For example, I might buy a car because it's fast and looks cool, while you might buy the same car because it's safe and reliable. If I tried to persuade you to buy the car by talking about its speed, that might be a turn-off to you. I don't know if you care about speed, but I'm assuming that you do because that's what *I* care about.

The egocentric persuader focuses on what *they* think should convince the person they're talking to rather than looking for what will *actually* convince the other person. They focus on the same path to persuasion they followed, and don't consider other ways to arrive at the same destination. But rather than considering adjustments when someone is unmoved by their approach, the egocentric persuader just writes the other person off as irrational, ignorant, or (when it comes to conversations about race) a racist or "liberal snowflake." When you use egocentric persuasion, you focus so much on yourself that you fail to see the needs of your conversational partner.

A basic thought exercise can illustrate why egocentric persuasion is so ineffective. Think about your current location. How would you tell me to get there? If you were to give me directions to where you are sitting at this moment, what would you say? Without knowing my current position, it is an impossible question to answer. How could you possibly give directions without a starting point? The path I take to reach you is going to be completely contingent upon where I am coming from. Likewise, egocentric persuasion ignores others' starting point.

Empathetic persuasion, on the other hand, recognizes that you can't effectively persuade another person unless you know where they're coming from. If you know I'm getting off the highway near your office, you can direct me to wherever you are. If I'm trying to convince you to buy a car, I'd have done better by first asking what you were looking for, and then tailoring my sales pitch to your needs.

If you ask your conversation partner questions and listen to what they're saying, they'll give you the key to unlocking the right path to persuading them. What is their history? What are their beliefs and values? What type of information resonates with them? Are they more persuaded by facts or feelings? Don't assume you know what will resonate with them; *ask them*.

Let's say that you believe that statues of Confederate soldiers should be torn down because, from your perspective, the people they honor were fighting to maintain the institution of slavery. Your colleague, on the other hand, believes that, even though they of course think slavery was wrong, they don't think that history should be destroyed, and tearing down the statues won't change the past.

YOU: Let's take a step back. You said that you don't believe the statues should be torn down because they are a reminder of history, right?

THEM: Yes, that's right. It's like people think tearing down these statues will change the past. It's not going to change anything.

YOU: Okay. I can agree with you that tearing the statues down won't change the past. We're not trying to rewrite history. Hypothetically, how would your perspective change if you knew that removing the statues could have a positive impact on the present and future?

THEM: But it doesn't.

YOU: Just humor me for a second. Hypothetically, how would your perspective change if you knew that removing the statues could have a positive impact on the present and future?

If someone doesn't answer my question, I'll often ask it again. If they dodge it a second time, I'll ask what's behind them dodging the question— because dodging relies on one of two things to be successful: the person who asked the question not recognizing that their question was dodged and proceeding without the information—or their giving up on getting the information. By addressing it directly instead, I'm letting them know that I recognized their dodge and I'm not letting it go.

THEM: I mean, yeah. If removing the statues had some kind of impact on the present and future, I'd consider tearing them down.

YOU: Okay, I appreciate that. So it sounds like the two main things you're concerned about in this circumstance are preserving history and the impact the statue has—whether or not removing the statues actually makes a difference. Is that a fair synopsis?

THEM: Yep, exactly.

This is a breakthrough moment in the conversation because they've just given you the answer to how to persuade them: you just need to convince them that removing the statues would have a positive impact.

YOU: Cool. Did you know that the statue in our town square wasn't put up right after the Civil War? It was put up in the 1920s.

THEM: Really?

YOU: Yeah. And, I mean, I don't need to tell you how badly Black Americans were treated in the 1920s.

THEM: No, I'm definitely with you there! There was still a lot of racism.

YOU: Right, I agree. And when you look at what was written on the statue, it isn't condemning what happened in the war.

THEM: That's true, it isn't.

YOU: Can you imagine being Black in this city in the 1920s and suddenly that statue, eulogizing a man who fought to keep people who looked like you enslaved—a statue that doesn't even acknowledge that slavery was wrong—gets erected?

THEM: I'd probably be pretty pissed. I wouldn't be happy.

YOU: Exactly. Now, how do you think some Black people *today* feel when people argue that we should leave it up?

THEM: Wow . . . okay. I never thought about it from that perspective. I just thought about it like a cool time capsule. I see what you're saying now. I still don't like the fact that it's eliminating history.

YOU: I feel you there. What would you propose to both respect our Black neighbors and condemn racism, while at the same time helping people to remember the past?

THEM: Uh, I guess if we start from scratch with a new monument that tells of the city's history but also shows how we've learned from it and we've changed to include everyone.

YOU: I think that could work.

What persuaded you—the fact that they were statues honoring Confederate war heroes—wasn't working to persuade your friend. So, instead of using egocentric persuasion, you used Compassionate Curiosity to identify what mattered to them—and then used that to persuade them, while also inviting them to consider solutions collaboratively.

MISTAKE #3: DISRESPECTING THE OTHER PERSON OR THEIR PERSPECTIVE

In *Crucial Conversations: Tools for Talking When Stakes Are High*, the authors describe the importance of respect in a conversation this way: "Respect is like air. As long as it's present, nobody thinks about it. But if you take it away, it's all that people can think about."[4] When you feel disrespected, you feel unappreciated, unseen, unheard. It can make you want to do or say something extreme to reassert yourself in the conversation—or give up on the interaction, and maybe the relationship, completely. Needless to say, that kind of dynamic makes it hard to communicate effectively.

Do you respect your conversation partner? I would guess that, in the majority of cases, both parties in difficult conversations would emphatically say yes, they respect the person they are speaking with. But do your actions, words, and thoughts communicate that respect? If your conversation partner makes a simple statement about feeling a certain way that you cannot understand, do you accept that, or do you question how they could possibly feel that way? Any time you discount what someone says about their feelings, or the impact their experience has had on their lives, you are not respecting them.

So, how do you show respect during these conversations? By listening. As former KKK leader Roger Kelly said about Daryl Davis, "I'd follow that man to hell and back because I believe in what he stands for and he believes in what I stand for. We don't agree with everything, but at least he respects me enough to sit down and listen to me, and I respect him enough to sit down and listen to him."

Respecting someone doesn't mean that you agree with everything they say, nor does it mean condoning inappropriate moral equivalencies, like comparing the Black Lives Matter Movement to the KKK (yes, I've actually heard this multiple times). What it does mean is that, regardless of whether or not you agree with the other person's perspective, you still respect them enough to listen.

Listening is something that most people struggle with. It's still tough for me, especially when I can feel my emotions rising. But listening is a skill that we can improve with time and practice, just like any other skill. One way to make practicing fun is by making it into a game. Give yourself a point if you can get the following to happen in your conversations over the course of the next week:

1. Get your conversation partner to say, "That's a great question!"
2. Get your conversation partner to say, "That's right," "Exactly," or, "You got it" after you summarize what they said.
3. Listen so well that your conversation partner asks you to share your thoughts (when you listen well, people want to reciprocate).

Do it again the week after, then compare your points to see if you improved.

MISTAKE #4: USING SHAME-BASED STRATEGIES

Author and researcher Brené Brown, PhD, describes shame as "the fear of disconnection—it's the fear that something we've done or failed to do, an ideal that we've not lived up to, or a goal that we've not accomplished makes us unworthy of connection."[5] A lot of people, whether intentionally or unintentionally, approach conversations in a way that makes it more likely for shame to take hold. And when shame enters the equation, it destroys any possibility of open conversation. The key to keeping shame from derailing your conversation is making the other person feel safe. If they don't feel safe in the conversation, then they won't feel comfortable being vulnerable enough to share information and meaningfully engage. They'll be guarded, and that will make it much more difficult for you to accomplish your goals.

Shame is not the same thing as guilt. Guilt, or the feeling that you have done something wrong, can be positive, because it can motivate you to rectify a situation. Shame, on the other hand, usually leads people to pull away from whatever triggered it, instead of focusing on solving the problem at hand.

A lot of conversations about race often seem to be *designed* to trigger shame. For example, just calling someone a racist is not a constructive comment. It's a label that is likely to trigger fear of disconnection or feelings that they are unworthy of connection. Most people will respond emotionally and defensively to such a label, and it will derail the conversation before substantive issues can be meaningfully addressed.

The conversation that Melanie, the Black woman I mentioned in chapter two, tried to have with the leaders of her company about issues of inclusivity is another example of a conversation about race triggering shame. The leaders' response induced shame because it invalidated Melanie's experience and those of her BIPOC colleagues without showing her the respect of meaningful consideration. By summarily dismissing and diminishing her contribution, they diminished her, too, making her feel "less than." Those feelings of shame led Melanie to protect herself by pulling back from the conversation, the relationship, and, ultimately, the company as a whole.

Shame rarely gets the outcome you're looking for. Brown's research suggests that people usually exhibit one of three responses to feelings of shame: moving away, moving toward, and moving against.

1. *Moving away* in response to shame involves avoiding discomfort by not thinking or talking about the source of that shame. This is where you might see people say, "We shouldn't be talking about race or racism at work."
2. *Moving toward* shame involves trying to people-please our way out of shame. This usually manifests in going along with ideas that we

don't agree with in order to keep the peace, while sacrificing our values and beliefs in the process.

3. *Moving against* shame means leveraging shame as a tool of destruction to fight back while causing pain in the process. Similar to fighting fire with fire, people using this tactic choose to fight shame with shame. This causes the conversation to spiral downward rapidly as shame, pain, and aggression take control.[6]

None of these responses is helpful for effective conversations. In the "best" of situations, when your approach causes someone to feel shame, they carry their wounds internally, withdrawing (moving away) or just acting like they agree with you out of fear in order to end the conversation as quickly as possible, which is a version of shame-induced people pleasing (moving toward). In the worst case, your conversation partner may become defensive, resistant, aggressive, vindictive, or even violent (moving against)—any of which make it much harder to connect with and persuade the other person. Also, if you make someone feel shame in a conversation, they're likely to associate that shame with you, which may poison your relationship.

No matter the *specific* outcome, the *general* outcome of using shame-based strategies is always that you immediately lose control of the conversation. Your carefully crafted strategy, designed to help you get closer to your "win," is ruined. In all my years of experience in psychology, influence, and persuasion, shame has never been a legitimate or effective way to persuade, connect, or communicate.

The Tenuous Balance Between Accountability and Shame

We need to hold people accountable for what they do and say. However, the process of holding someone accountable, especially on race-related issues, potentially can trigger shame. You can't control another person's emotions. The challenge in this case is to do what you can to mitigate their feelings of shame without excusing their words or behavior.

Although you *can't* control whether someone feels shame associated with what they've said, done, or believed in the past, you *can* control whether you use a shame-based approach—whether you are saying *they* are bad, or whether you're saying they merely *did* something bad.

A redemptive approach holds the other person accountable while letting them know that, although what they did hurt or is hurting others, you do not believe they are a bad person or that they intended to cause offense. They can still find redemption. This makes it more likely that they will mobilize the inevitable uncomfortable emotions such a conflict stirs up internally for positive change and personal growth.

One of the things that causes people to "armor up" and get defensive in conversations where they are being held accountable is their fear that, if they concede that they made a mistake or harbored problematic beliefs, they won't be able to recover from it professionally or socially. They've seen people get "canceled" and they don't want to become a pariah, be labeled racist, or worse. So instead of focusing on their own problematic actions and beliefs, they focus on you and what they perceive as your problematic approach.

They'll also associate you with the shame that they feel, eroding the relationship and making them resistant to anything you say in the future. This will make reflexive rejection more likely, because they will want to protect themselves from more damage. In short, when you deploy a shame-based approach in your attempts to hold people accountable, you've just made your job harder. *You can't shame someone into being an ally.*

Creating trust and psychological safety in these conversations doesn't mean that we're coddling people and protecting them from all emotional discomfort. Often, protecting people from challenging emotions will be antithetical to what you're trying to accomplish. Still, although discomfort is often a natural byproduct of the conversation, it should never be the explicit goal. You want to let the other person know that, within this conversation, they are safe to transform, they are safe to wrestle with the complexities and difficulties of the situation, and they are safe to realize that they made a mistake.

Shame and Word Choice

Being effective in difficult conversations about race means that you have to consider not only what you say, but also how you say it. And whether or not you're saying something in the right way depends completely on your goals. Always ask yourself: *Does crafting my message this way take me closer to or farther from my goals?*

One of the tips that my mentor, Mark Decker, gave me was that you never call a liar a liar in a negotiation, because once you call someone a liar, you've destroyed the relationship. Liars and honest people have something in common: they both hate being called liars. And it's hard to have a productive conversation after you've given someone a label they feel emotionally and strategically obligated to forcefully reject.

In this case, the word *liar* is an example of what, in negotiation parlance, is known as a *trigger word*. These are words that tend to create defensiveness in the form of reflexive rejection and are likely to cause an unproductive conversational detour. At best, they derail the conversation; at worst, they irreparably damage the relationship. The good news is there is almost always an alternative word that allows you to get your point across without the strategic risk. Whenever I see another valid option to communicate my message, I take it, because I'm not married to the words I use in the conversation; I'm married to the outcome.

In conversations about race, the word *racist* is a trigger word.

Let's pause for a moment and review some realities. Racism is real. Racists are real. And people should be held accountable for racism. I recognize that sometimes the use of the terms *racism* and *racist* is unavoidable. But remember, we're operating under the assumption that, because you and your conversation partner share a workplace, you at least need to come out of the discussion able to work together. *Regardless of the veracity of the claim, labeling your peers, or your organization, with the term* racist *during the conversation will rarely lead to the outcome you're trying to achieve.* (This is assuming, of course, that your aim is meaningful engagement on the topic.) Once someone has been labeled racist, they're likely going to spend the rest of the conversation defending themselves, rather than working with you to solve the problem at hand.[7]

Very few people will simply accept the label of *racist*, either for themselves or their actions. As a result, using the word means the conversation is almost guaranteed to go so far off of the conversational highway that you'll never find a return route to productive dialogue. Also, since many people perceive racism as requiring malicious intent, they will respond with the legitimate claim that they are the only person privy to the inner workings of their mind, and *they know* they weren't being malicious. The conversation then becomes especially unproductive because now you're having an argument about what is or is not in their head.

Fortunately, there are ways to avoid this predictable barrier while still delivering a message that is accurate, clear, and assertive—to achieve the same goal *without* labeling people in a way that makes it less likely a productive conversation will result.

Think back to chapter four's formula for starting a difficult conversation—*situation + impact + invitation = engaged communication*—and how, in describing the situation and the impact, it's most effective to use naked facts that are completely without judgment and interpretation. What I've found in establishing the situation and impact in difficult conversations about race is that it's better to use terms like *racially inequitable impact* or *racialized outcome* than *racist* or *racism*. This means saying something like:

> *I've discovered that BIPOC employees within our organization earn, on average, 13 percent less than their White counterparts. I believe that this is happening, in large part, because of several policies that are creating racially inequitable outcomes.*

Versus:

> *We have several racist policies within our organization that are leading to inequitable racist outcomes.*

The former approach allows you to clearly communicate your message without losing efficacy.

Again, I'm not saying that the terms *racist* and *racism* should be *completely* avoided. Sometimes there's no other way to describe what's happening. What I'm saying is that we should be intentional about how and when we use them. Whether you use them and how depend completely on the circumstances, your audience, and your goals. Know your audience, anticipate their response, and then determine your strategy appropriately.

Not using the word *racism* as a label also often *improves* the clarity of your message. Whether something is technically "racist" is largely subjective, because different people define racism differently (remember the section on semantic arguments earlier in this chapter?). For example, many people subscribe to the belief that the term *racist* is, as author Ibram X. Kendi notes, "merely descriptive" and "not pejorative,"[8] whereas others believe that the term *racist* is a synonym for *evil* and is one of the most damning labels in society. Even if *you* believe the term is merely descriptive, when you label someone as racist, they will understand the label through *their own* definition. We filter our world through our biases and emotions before we filter it through rational thought.[9] Thus, even if we explain that we didn't mean offense, we already will have offended.

Fortunately, using a trigger word is rarely our only option. The facts of a situation—the action or words in question, and the harm they caused—are absolute; the words we use to describe the situation are much more flexible. Another way I get around using words like *racist* or *racism* is by describing the impact or outcomes of the situation, rather than offering my subjective judgment about the situation.

Again, we *are not* letting people off the hook. We *are* holding people and organizations accountable. We're just doing it using an approach that makes it more likely that they will engage and the conversation will be productive.

Recently, I worked with the leader of a mid-sized company who had received a number of race-related complaints from employees about various coworkers. The CEO had started the company as a solo shop and grown it rapidly over the previous decade, and was deeply troubled by what was happening in his organization. The director of HR asked ANI to evaluate the situation and help the staff reconcile their differences.

The CEO was reluctant to engage in the process because someone had written an anonymous blog post accusing him and the organization of being racist. He was terrified of saying or doing something wrong, and his fear was leading him to completely avoid any conversations addressing race or racism in his company. His discomfort and avoidance stalled any chance of progress, because those addressing the problem needed his blessing to proceed.

After staying in level one communication for the entirety of our first meeting and half of our second, he started to feel more comfortable sharing. He said that when he was growing up, his father called Martin Luther King Jr. a troublemaker and accused him of creating more problems than he was solving. And he himself never thought there were any problems regarding race because when he looked around his community, everything was fine and people were happy. Initially, the same was true at his little company, and he had no clue there was a problem. He felt embarrassed about it, and was resistant to making changes because he was confused about why these problems were occurring and what could possibly be done about them. His approach and his fears had led him to avoid having the important but difficult conversations needed for his company to progress.

I've found that, when I have conversations with clients or peers in the professional world, they will spend a lot of time discussing diversity, equity, and inclusion in their company, as if they are trying to convince me of their good intentions. It is an emotional need that can be a distraction if not properly acknowledged. In negotiation, taking the time to acknowledge those good intentions is an example of what's called an *emotional payment*. It costs me nothing, means the world to them, and allows me to shift their focus from trying to convince me they're not a problem to how they can be part of the solution.[10] It's not something I always feel like doing in the moment, but I've found that it increases the likelihood of productive dialogue without sacrificing my ultimate goal.

Here, I told the CEO, "Given your lived experience, it would be tough for you to fully understand the situation. We can't change the past, but we can change the future. Now that you have a better understanding of what's happening, we have an opportunity to make things better."

After our conversations, he was much more open and receptive. He apologized to his staff, vowed to do better, and asked them to hold him accountable. That made everybody feel a lot more comfortable having these conversations, and they were able to work together in order to make the appropriate changes.

This example demonstrates how we need to design our approach for meaningful engagement. Using trigger words and then calling the other person "fragile" while blaming them for the lack of productive dialogue is assuming a position of powerlessness. We have more control over outcomes in these conversations than it might seem. Instead of using language that makes people feel bad about *themselves*, make them feel bad about the *problem* and show them how they can be part of the solution.

MISTAKE #5: USING ABSOLUTES

One of the simplest rules of difficult conversations is to refrain from absolutes. These statements usually include words like *always*, *never*, and *every*.

Unless you're discussing the immutable laws of physics, our world involves very few absolutes. Using them therefore invites people to exploit the vulnerabilities in your argument. All your conversation partner has to do is find a single instance of what you said not being true, and your entire argument falls apart. Then, instead of discussing the topic at hand, the argument becomes whether what you said is true *always* or *some of the time*.

I frequently witness these types of arguments break down in conversations about race and racism. For example, one person says racism is embedded within *every* inch of America. That might be true—and it might not be true. How would we prove it? Suddenly the conversation shifts to whether racism is embedded in all, some, or few areas of the American experience.

To avoid finding yourself in a similar situation, ask yourself:

- What is my goal?
- Can I achieve that goal *without* using superlatives that are vulnerable to attack?

Whenever you're trying to persuade someone, you should anticipate and address counterpoints. When you make an absolute statement, the counterpoints are predictable, and, quite frankly, don't even need to be that good to undermine your credibility in the other person's eyes. This will make persuasion harder, both now and in the future. The good news is, you rarely need to speak in absolutes. There is usually an alternative way to make your point that's both more persuasive and resistant to attack.

For example:

- **Instead of *always*, use *often*.** *Our BIPOC colleagues are* always *treated unjustly* versus *Our BIPOC colleagues are* often *treated unjustly.*
- **Instead of *will*, use *likely* or *frequently*.** *If we don't change this policy it* will *have a detrimental impact on our DEI goals* versus *If we don't change this policy it's* likely *to have a detrimental impact on our DEI goals.*
- **Instead of *never*, use *rarely* or *infrequently*.** *Our company has* never *made strategic decisions with equity in mind* versus *Our company has* rarely *made strategic decisions with equity in mind.*

These minor adjustments allow you to still speak truthfully and powerfully without setting yourself up for being derailed.

MISTAKE #6: UNDERESTIMATING THE POWER OF EMOTIONS

Most people don't struggle with having feelings; they struggle with strategizing and executing. This is why most of the book focuses on the latter two. But the strategic approach presented in this book is not about denying your emotions or muting them; it's about channeling them in productive ways.

Strong emotions are like nuclear energy: they're incredibly powerful, and can be used either productively or destructively. Whether we are successful in using our emotional power is determined by control. We want to make sure we're in control of our emotions, rather than letting our emotions control us. A well-timed and mindfully-placed display of passion can be incredibly persuasive. But when it comes to strategy, it's all about using the right tool at the right time. Even though I'm passionate and have strong feelings about a topic, I need to exert emotional discipline to make sure I channel that passion in persuasive ways. That's where internally directed Compassionate Curiosity comes into play. It helps me to self-regulate so I can manage my emotions effectively during the conversation.

One of my good friends and mentors, Judge Laurel Beatty Blunt, shared a story on the *Negotiate Anything* podcast that perfectly exemplifies the importance of managing your emotions.[11] One time an attorney went on a lengthy and insulting rant during a hearing in which they criticized Judge Beatty Blunt's capabilities. She was furious, but she didn't let her emotions take her off track. Especially feeling the need to be mindful of not fulfilling negative stereotypes as a Black judge, she chose to pause instead of responding right away.

"After he went on his tirade, and it was a tirade, I sat there and I just let several different inappropriate responses that honestly had expletives in them go through my head." The pause lasted over a minute. Then, she "just looked up and calmly responded to him and said, 'Your insults are not persuasive. Is there anything further, counsel?'" And then the hearing was over. She described it as a "mic drop moment." If she had, instead, responded reflexively with cathartic communication, then she would have missed out on an opportunity to demonstrate her control over the proceeding, while protecting the relationship from further damage in the process.

In my experience, appeals to emotion are most persuasive *after* you've worked through your conversation partner's challenging emotions. I think of this as making space for the emotional state I want them to be in. When the other person is frustrated, annoyed, scared, or feeling other strong emotions, it's more difficult for them to experience any different emotional state. However, if I use Compassionate Curiosity to lower their emotional temperature, it's easier for me to lead them to a more productive emotional state.

If you find you are struggling to lower the temperature on your conversation partner's emotions, you may have better luck just refocusing them. DEI discussions can be especially difficult because the people involved tend to have passionate views based in morality. In his episode of ANI's *Negotiate Anything* podcast, psychology professor and researcher Andrew Luttrell shared that the more passionate a person is, the harder it is to persuade them using data alone. Their confirmation bias allows them to come up with an endless number of counterpoints. However, if you try to persuade them to *feel* strongly about the problem you're presenting, you are likely to find more success. Essentially, you want to replace their current strongly-held beliefs with new strongly-held beliefs.

For example, let's say the person you're talking to believes that America is the land of opportunity and everybody has an equal chance to succeed, and when you challenge that belief, they get upset. You could say something like, "Yes, you should feel strongly about this because this is America and that's how it should be for everybody. The problem is, it's not. We have the same vision for what we want America to be, and there are certain changes that need to happen in order to make that vision a reality. As Americans, we can't stand for this." You aren't trying to change their beliefs, or asking them not to feel strongly. You're just refocusing their passion by helping them to adjust the specifics.

MISTAKE #7: TRYING TO CHANGE HOW THE OTHER PERSON THINKS ABOUT *EVERYTHING*

The Human Genome Project was an ambitious marvel of science. Researchers were able to sequence and map all the genes in the human genome. One of the most fascinating findings was how similar our genome is to those of other animals: for example, humans and chimps share 96 percent of their DNA.[12] Genetically speaking, by changing a little, you can change a lot.

A similar concept applies in persuasion. In difficult conversations, we're trying to find what I like to call "the Genetic Code of Beliefs": what allows the other person to believe what they believe. In my experience, as with the human genetic code, if you can change a person's beliefs just a little bit, you can change a lot about their behavior.

Frequently in these conversations, we make the mistake of trying to change the other person's entire genetic code—a Herculean task. Not only is this unlikely to succeed, but also, most importantly, it's unnecessary. You don't need to change a person's entire belief system in order to change their perspective on the issue at hand. Often you only need to change a very small portion of it.

For example, the board members of a large consulting firm in the South were considering bringing ANI in for a series of DEI trainings and strategic consulting. The younger members of the board wanted to move forward with the program we proposed, but they couldn't proceed without the blessing of a few of the older members, who were hesitant because they were afraid our trainings would be too "political" and "divisive."

I spent forty-five minutes listening to the older board members' Genetic Code of Beliefs so I could understand their broader concerns about the company and what they wanted to accomplish. The linchpin for persuading your conversation partner will often be found in a set of beliefs adjacent to—but not directly touching—the topic at hand. In this case, I learned that a major concern for them was the future of the consulting firm. I asked them a few targeted questions designed to understand their goals and expand their perspective:

- When people look at your company's team page, how much diversity do they see?
- When you look at the webpages of your various competitors, how much diversity do you see?
- Especially given that your client base is diversifying, what message does the lack of diversity on your team send to your potential clients?
- If your consultants aren't culturally competent, how will they connect with your clients?

Once I had linked our trainings to the company's future success, it didn't take long for the older members to get on board. A few short minutes later, one of them said, "If we don't get this right, it could be an existential threat to our company. We're going to struggle to recruit, we're going to struggle to get new clients, and we're going to struggle to compete."

Did their underlying belief system regarding DEI and race in America change? No. Did it have to? No. All that had to change was how they thought about what was best for the future of the company—a very specific issue that meant a lot to them. Changing that small part of their Genetic Code of Beliefs led to a cascade of different behaviors and lasting structural changes. In less than a year, they had:

- conducted a series of trainings,
- created and began executing an ambitious strategic plan for DEI,
- significantly increased the racial and gender diversity of their staff, and
- hired a woman to be the leader of the company for the first time in its storied history.

Change can't happen without persuasive communication—but the change in beliefs required to create a change in behavior doesn't have to be as significant as you might think.

ONE FINAL NOTE

The mistakes described in this chapter are not the only ones that you can, or will, make during difficult conversations. The good news—and the thing I most want you to take away from this—is that if you listen, interpret what someone is saying with an open mind, and temper your responses with an eye toward developing or maintaining the relationship, you can weather almost any mistake.

DISCUSSION QUESTIONS

- Is there a mistake you have made in a difficult conversation that is not covered in this chapter? If so, what was it and how did you handle the situation? How will you handle it in the future?
- How do you define respect? When was the last time you felt a lack of respect from someone, and what did they do to make you feel that way?
- How will you avoid the mistakes in this chapter in your next difficult conversation?
- Can you identify any biases that would cause you to make one of these mistakes? If so, how can you overcome that bias during your next difficult conversation?

PART THREE

Taking Action

HOW TO BE AN ADVOCATE
FOR POSITIVE CHANGE

f a tree falls in the woods and nobody hears it, did it really make a sound?"
I always thought this was a silly question. My response was always,
"Who cares?" But if we replace a few words, we get a very different question:
If an advocate isn't able to create positive change, are they really an advo-
cate? If you call yourself an advocate, but your words and actions don't lead
to any meaningful change, then are you really an advocate?

The difference between being an advocate and being an ally can be
confusing. I've found this definition from online training company Mursion
quite helpful: "Think of these words not as nouns, but as verbs, and the
distinction become[s] clearer: To ally yourself with someone or something
is to associate, join, or unite; to advocate is to speak or write in favor of,
to support by argument, or to recommend publicly."[1] The term *advocate* is
more appropriate for the purposes of this book because it focuses on taking
action using persuasion and influence *regardless of your racial identity*.

Advocate isn't just a title; it's a verb. Whether or not you deserve the moniker depends on whether you're able to actually create positive change. And an essential part of being able to create change is how active a role you are taking in persuading the people around you.

This doesn't mean you have to seek out every possible opportunity to talk about race. Oftentimes, the topic will come up unexpectedly. If you're a leader in an organization, these conversations can become necessary in the normal course of doing business, and you need to answer the call. These situations are more *reactive*. But being an advocate means being ready to use the powerful tools you've learned from this book when the opportunity arises to create positive change and work toward racial equity within your organization.

MAXIMIZE YOUR IMPACT

If you want to maximize your impact, start with this simple truth: *racial inequity is a problem of bad policy, not bad people.*[2] Don't focus on changing people; focus on changing inequitable policies that create inequitable outcomes. You will get a greater return on investment if you focus on the policies that shape an organization, rather than the personal beliefs of the individuals within it.

To create meaningful, lasting change, you have to change behaviors. As James Clear, author of *Atomic Habits,* has noted, "You do not rise to the level of your goals, you fall to the levels of your systems."[3] For example, let's say you have a messy desk. You can take a day to clean it off, and afterward, it will look immaculate. Congratulations—mission accomplished! But for how long? Unless you change the habits that led to the messy desk in the first place, your desk is just going to get messy again.

Policy change must be priority number one. And although people's feelings and beliefs are important and should be taken into consideration, you cannot always wait for people to change before you act. Progress doesn't move at the speed of comfort. If we wait for everyone to feel comfortable, we'll wait forever. We can't merely hope that things will get better over time without taking action. I've said it before, and I'll say it again: hope (alone) is not a strategy. In the words of Martin Luther King Jr., "Human progress never rolls in on wheels of inevitability, but comes from continuous struggle."

Interestingly enough, policy change can be the very thing that changes hearts and minds. In other words, structural change often precedes moral change. For example, the Supreme Court ruling in *Brown v. Board of Education* that led to the integration of schools was hugely unpopular, especially among White people, at the time of the decision. But in the decades after the policy change, White support soared.[4] In 1958, only 4 percent of Americans approved of marriages between Black and White people. Then, in 1967, the Supreme Court ruled that laws banning interracial marriages were unconstitutional, and by 2013, 87 percent of Americans approved of Black–White marriages.[5]

During the COVID-19 pandemic, organizations learned that they can pivot a lot faster than they thought they could. For example, at the beginning of 2020, Florida A&M University had only 10 percent of their courses available online, with plans to get 25 percent of their courses online within two years. The pandemic forced them to get 100 percent of their courses online in roughly one week.[6]

We can make changes very quickly if we believe they're worth it. During the pandemic, companies' cost–benefit analyses showed that the benefit of massive change outweighed the cost of staying the same. The changes they made were tough, their initial solutions often imperfect, but they knew the challenges were worth it.

Necessity is the mother of invention. We are incredibly adaptable when we deem adaptation necessary to our survival. When organizations aren't willing to make changes to create more racial equity, it's a sign that they don't believe it's worth it. So don't feel bad pushing your organization to do better.

There will be resistance; that's to be expected, and we'll talk about how to overcome that resistance throughout the chapter. For the moment, though, I'll just challenge you to do this: ask radical questions. We often don't have massive success because we don't set massive goals. And setting massive goals starts with daring to ask more ambitious questions.

For example, I was working with a group of public health professionals who said they wanted to reduce infant mortality by 10 percent over the next three years. Curious, I asked, "Why not one year?" They paused for a moment, then said they weren't exactly sure why they didn't choose something more aggressive. I often find it helpful to ask challenging questions hypothetically, because hypotheticals feel less threatening than questions that require people to wrestle with reality. Plus, as I mentioned earlier in the book, hypotheticals can also trigger greater curiosity. So I then asked a follow-up: "Hypothetically, what would it take for us to reduce the infant mortality rate by 10 percent in one year?" The question sparked new levels of creative, resourceful thinking.

The quality of the answers we receive is contingent upon the quality of the questions we ask. Asking challenging questions that force people to think more aggressively can yield remarkable answers. Then, it's usually not a question of whether or not those changes can be implemented but instead of whether or not we have the collective will to make them happen.

USE YOUR LEVERAGE

Leverage is the ability to compel the other side to move closer to your position. The more leverage you have, the more you can get from the other side.

One of the easiest ways to determine leverage is to ask yourself this simple question: Who needs the deal the most? The side with the greatest need is the side with the least leverage.

Over the course of history, people have often struggled with how to create positive social change when (they *perceive* that) they don't have any power. Trying to create change when you seem to lack authority can feel daunting. However, as G. Richard Shell notes in his book *Bargaining for Advantage*, people often mistakenly consider power and leverage to be the same thing. "Leverage is about situational advantage, not objective power. Parties with very little conventional power can have a lot of leverage under the right circumstances."[7] As an advocate for positive change in your organization, *you have much more leverage than you think.*

For the purposes of this section, we're going to focus on three sources of leverage: positive, negative, and societal. Positive leverage comes from understanding what the other side wants and finding ways to give it to them—for example, if an employee performs well, then they get a bonus. The bonus is something they want, so they adjust their behavior in order to acquire it.

Negative leverage comes from understanding what the other side *doesn't* want and creating scenarios for them that avoid it—for example if your child doesn't finish their homework on time, then they can't watch TV over the weekend. The punishment is something your child would like to avoid, so they adjust their behavior.

Last, *societal leverage* comes from existing standards, shifting cultural norms, and the zeitgeist of the day. Think of it as grassroots power of the people, achieved through growing numbers of supporters or the accumulation of cultural momentum.

One of the best examples of the strategic use of societal leverage is Mahatma Gandhi's movement to secure independence for India from the British. India is a linguistically, ethnically, and socially diverse country inhabited by different communities with different experiences and agendas. Gandhi convinced them to temporarily set aside their individual struggles and refocus on the underlying aspiration they all held—freedom from colonization—so that they could utilize their collective power against the British. These different communities worked together in several nonviolent protests that pressured the British government to come to the negotiation table. Yes, this incredibly oversimplifies the history of Indian independence. But it illustrates how powerful societal leverage can be. Gandhi's leverage increased with each person who joined his movement. As the overall numbers and cumulative support grew, so too did his ability to persuade the British government.

Effective persuasion usually incorporates elements of all three, focusing primarily on positive and societal leverage versus negative leverage. For example, let's say you work for a manufacturing company and there have been numerous complaints of racist behavior: specifically, people using racial epithets on the plant floor and bias in promotion. You have tried repeatedly to address the issue, but leadership has failed to make it a priority, so nothing has been done for more than six months. The following are examples of how you could use all three forms of leverage in your persuasive strategy:

Positive leverage. Gather research that indicates that if this problem is addressed, the company could increase plant's productivity and efficiency. For example, addressing this issue could lead to fewer distractions and improved communication, increasing productivity and thus, potentially, company profits.

Negative leverage. Let's say your research finds that a significant percentage of the lawsuits faced by the company are brought by employees and center on race-related issues—and the company has to devote more than $50,000 annually per plant to legal expenses. By addressing this issue, the company could avoid significant legal fees.

Societal leverage. Conduct a poll to see how many people on the factory floor would like these issues to be addressed. If a high percentage of your colleagues see this as a significant issue that needs immediate attention, then you could use that persuasively in your future conversations.

Leverage is dynamic, not static—the power dynamics in your negotiations will shift with their circumstances.[8] Because of this constant shift, one of the most important considerations when wielding societal leverage is timing.

For instance, in 2020, there was a massive push for diversity, equity, and inclusion after the murder of George Floyd and the social unrest that followed. Some companies did quickly make changes as a result, but others watched from the sidelines and waited before making any decisions. The changemakers within those slow-moving companies ultimately struggled to get them to commit to doing *anything*, because the more time that passed, and the more the emotional fervor started to die down, *the less societal leverage they had.* They lost their leverage and, with it, their opportunity to create change. Whenever you realize that there is widespread recognition of the value or necessity of change within your organization, whatever the reason, you have to move quickly.

Although the various forms of leverage can make advocating for change easier, they aren't, on their own, enough. One of the biggest emotional barriers mentioned by changemakers in a variety of industries is the completely legitimate feeling that they *should not need to* negotiate equity and justice—that people should do the right thing because it is the right thing to do. But even when everyone agrees change is necessary, making change happen almost always requires a push. And if we put the responsibility of change in the hands of others, we are giving away our power, which leads to the predictable outcome of disappointment and frustration.

The responsibility for advancing liberty and justice is *yours.* You cannot afford the luxury of believing that someone else will take up the mantle. You must treat advocacy as if it is your personal responsibility to create change. Remember, you have more leverage than you think. You *can* create positive change in your organization if you blend the leverage that you *do* have with the right strategic approach.

PROTECTING YOUR MENTAL HEALTH

Advocacy is a never-ending journey toward positive change, which can be emotionally and psychologically taxing. Knowing when to take a step back and protect yourself is an act of radical self-love. So while viewing advocacy as your personal responsibility is important for ensuring you act, you also have to remember that you can't be an effective advocate when you're sidelined due to burnout. Finding balance is key.

One of the things I personally struggled with when it came to advocacy early in my career was the continuous news cycle. I was watching too much news, and it was making me hyper-aware of the negative things in the world and in society. I felt a lot of stress, and it became difficult for me to enjoy other aspects of my life because I was *too* aware of the negative: my constant consumption of negativity had primed my brain to see negativity constantly. Yet although I became much happier when I stopped watching the news completely, I wasn't well enough informed to have the positive impact on the world that I wanted to have. It made me feel better, but it wasn't helping me actually *be* better.

I had to create a different approach, one that worked for me. Now, if two people that I respect mention the same news story, then I look into it; otherwise, I ignore it. I prefer to consume news by reading whenever possible; after the murder of George Floyd, the graphic images dominated every news channel and social media platform nonstop, but I chose not to watch the video or look at the photos because I didn't need to traumatize myself—I just needed information.

I use what I call the *triangulation of the truth* to look for commonalities between different versions of the same story, to get closer to understanding what *actually* happened. And before I start to absorb the opinions of others, I try to formulate my own opinion of what happened and why.

This works for me, but it might not necessarily work for you. When I shared my approach with one of my friends, a White ally who lives in Minnesota, they said that although they respected my method, it wouldn't work for them: "You are a Black male living in America. Racism has affected you in a very personal way so it makes sense to try to protect yourself. For me, on the other hand, I've lived a very privileged life. I need to feel this. I need to experience this in order to empathize more effectively and understand what other people are going through."

In medicine, there is what's known as the "minimum effective dose." Doctors want you to take medicine, but no more than is necessary to address the disease, because then you could get hurt. We should apply the same mentality to consuming the news and staying informed. Determine what approach allows you to stay informed without taking too much of a toll on your mental health. I can't tell you where that line is—that's something that you need to determine for yourself.

Advocacy is hard; it's important to figure out how to do it without damaging yourself in the process. Nandini Malhotra, our amazing research associate, often quotes the wisdom of the Talmud when considering its challenges:

> *Do not be daunted by the enormity of the world's grief.*
> *Do justly, now.*
> *Love mercy, now.*
> *Walk humbly, now.*
> *You are not obligated to complete the work, but neither are you free to abandon it.*

BEND THE RULES (ETHICALLY, OF COURSE)

On my first day of law school, one of my professors posed an interesting hypothetical: "Imagine you're making a case in front of a judge or jury and you are given a choice—you can choose either all of the facts that are presented in the case or all of the rules that apply to the case. Which would you choose to guarantee a victory for your client?"

Most of us said that we would choose the facts. We believed it would be more advantageous to be able to choose every piece of evidence that would be seen by the judge and jury. Our professor smiled smugly and said, "What do you do when I choose the rules, and my rules say that your facts don't matter?"

As an eager advocate, it's easy to believe that your facts will win the day. Since they are compelling to you, you assume that they will be compelling to others (remember confirmation bias and egocentric persuasion?).[9] But just as in the hypothetical, the "rules" of your company may dictate that your facts don't matter.

In law, there's something called the *burden of proof*, where the party bringing a case to trial is the one responsible for providing evidence and persuading the decision maker. If you're trying to create positive change in your company, the burden of proof is on *you*. It's your responsibility to make your case and persuade others to do what you want them to do. Leadership needs to reach a level of certainty about the need for a particular change before it is willing to proceed. And when you know the rules—when you know what your company needs in order to feel certain change is needed—you're better equipped to make your case.

Does this kind of resistance sound familiar to you?

You can't prove that.
That's unscientific.
Why jump to racism when it could be so many other things?
How do we know for sure that this is the right way to do it?
Are we sure this is a good investment?

When you identify racial inequity in your company and try to do something about it, you likely will encounter a lot of skepticism, criticism, and resistance. Anticipate this—in fact, invite it. After all, a critical eye can often reveal your blind spots, and the collaborative process can make your solutions even more potent.

Often, however, this potentially beneficial process gets off track as, intentionally or not, people keep moving the goalposts. They claim that they need more evidence in order to be convinced, and then, when you provide that evidence, for some reason that evidence is insufficient as well.

How often do you have the luxury of being *completely certain* before making a decision? In many aspects of life, complete certainty is not a realistic possibility. And, as such, it's rarely required in order to make decisions. For example, in the United States legal system, the hundreds of thousands of civil cases each year are decided by a standard called the *preponderance of the evidence*. Under this standard, all you need to do is convince a judge or jury that there is a greater than 50 percent chance that the person on trial committed the act in question.[10]

When you look at decision-making norms in the business world, there is a fundamental understanding that business involves risk, and that risk comes from the fact that it's nearly impossible to understand everything with absolute certainty. If the business standard was to wait for complete certainty to act, there would never be any action. The same will be true as you make the case for change within your organization.

People will often try to hold you to increasingly unrealistic standards as you make your case. To avoid this, pre-negotiate the terms of the agreement. Before you begin gathering evidence and making your case, negotiate for valid and legitimate decision-making standards. Here's an example of what that could look like:

YOU: Like I mentioned before, a number of BIPOC employees in the organization are concerned about pay discrepancies and opportunities to advance. If those exist, then we need to do something about it.

THEM: Agreed. Do some research and get back to us.

YOU: Okay, before I do that, I need to get some clarification from you about what you're looking for. What will you need to see in order to commit to making changes?

THEM: I don't know. Just show me what you come up with and we'll see.

YOU: The problem is that I need to know what kind of data you're looking for. For example, if I come back with a qualitative survey and you're looking for hard statistical data, then we just wasted a lot of time. So, what specifically would you need to see?

THEM: Yeah, surveys don't do it for me. It would need to be something more concrete. I'd need to see data broken down by race, gender, years of experience, and productivity.

YOU: Thank you for that. That makes sense. If we want that kind of information, we're going to need to bring someone in to conduct the assessment, and also get the CFO involved with the project because she's the one who has the data and we'll need to talk about the budget.

THEM: Okay. Have a meeting with the CFO and keep me posted.

YOU: One last thing before I go. How much of a discrepancy do you need to see for you to be willing to make changes?

THEM: Any discrepancy outside of the margin of error is unacceptable.

After that conversation, put the terms in writing by sending the other parties an email that recaps the entire interaction. Then you can move forward in the process with confidence because you know what it will take to make the case.

NEGOTIATE REAL CHANGE

On ANI's *Negotiate Real Change* podcast, we highlight leaders who are changing their companies using a blend of negotiation, conflict resolution, and change management skills. The more we talked to leaders in the diversity, equity, and inclusion space, the more we started to recognize the patterns of successful changemakers within organizations. Because of this new understanding of what it takes to be successful advocates, ANI developed a new approach for guiding companies through structural change, which we call the *Negotiate Real Change Model*. It's a simple three-step framework:

1. Gather and analyze data
2. Create a strategic approach
3. Execute the strategy

We think of this as a success cycle because it should be repeated until you are successful—in other words, it repeats as long as inequity persists within the organization.

Here's an example of what this looks like in action. After the social unrest during the summer of 2020, changemakers within NBBJ, an industry-leading architecture firm, started having conversations with each other. They used what was happening outside of the company to spark important discussions within the company and asked themselves, "What can we do to make our organization more equitable and have a greater positive impact on society?"

They weren't sure what to do next, so they reached out to ANI for help. We started by using step one of the Negotiate Real Change Model, gathering and analyzing the data. To do this, we conducted a customized company-wide DEI assessment to understand the employees' perspectives. Then we moved to step two, creating a strategic plan. Using our findings, we worked collaboratively with the leadership to create a DEI strategy that included DEI trainings, a plan to increase diversity within the firm, and community engagement. One of my favorite parts of the plan is called "Design Justice." It recognizes how the actual architectural design of a building can promote diversity, equity, and inclusion. A major part of the initiative is a commitment to "challenge structural inequalities and use design to sustain, heal and restore marginalized communities."[11] Lastly, and most importantly, NBBJ promptly moved to the third step: execution.

Having specific, objective metrics is important. The mistake that a lot of companies make is ending their DEI conversations with nebulous aspirations like, "We will make the company more diverse." While this is a good start, on its own it isn't enough. How will you know you've achieved your goal?

The most effective goals—the ones that are most likely to lead to change—are SMART goals: goals that are Specific, Measurable, Achievable, Relevant, and Time-Bound. In other words, you need your goals to be concrete. For example, NBBJ created specific success metrics for their DEI strategy and shared them with the entire staff. This made it clear to everyone in the organization where they currently were and where they wanted to be. When you make concrete goals and state them publicly, then people inside and outside of your organization can hold you accountable. This greatly increases the likelihood that you will meet those goals.

If you are a change agent within your organization and you want to learn how you can create your own program using our approach, you can download our free *Negotiate Real Change* guide at www.americannegotiationinstitute.com/negotiation-guides.

PERFECT IS UNREALISTIC; FOCUS ON BETTER

When it comes to creating a just and equitable multicultural society, we are, in many ways, building the plane as we fly it. No society has managed to solve racism. The problem is that, in many cases, we drag our feet on making progress because we can't find the "perfect solution." But the perfect solution *doesn't exist*. Don't focus on perfect; focus on better. Don't focus exclusively on the flaws of the proposed solution; focus on whether it gets us closer to our ultimate goals.

CREATE FERTILE SOIL

Once, when talking to a fellow mediator who worked in the same court system I did, I asked them, "What do you do when the topic of race comes up in your mediations?"

They looked at me, confused, thought for a second, then responded, "I've done hundreds of mediations, but the topic of race has never come up."

I was shocked! The subject of race and/or unfair treatment because of race had been brought up many times in my mediations, and it was never a surprise to hear.

Similarly, I was facilitating a mediation case for a police department in the Southwest concerning a racial issue where the chief told me, "We are proud to say that in the last five years, we haven't had any race-related complaints." Unable to hide the surprise on my face, I said, "The person I'm talking to in the other room just mentioned three other specific incidents that they were aware of personally—in addition to what we're talking about today."

I can't tell you how many times I've heard company leaders, in a strategy session after reviewing the findings of their assessments for the first time, express how completely devastated they were. I regularly hear people say things like "This breaks my heart" and "Why didn't people tell us they felt this way before? We had no idea." These kinds of surprises are less likely to occur when organizations create an atmosphere that encourages, rather than discourages, difficult conversations about race.

A lot of times when BIPOC do talk about their challenges in the workplace, other people try to convince them that what happened didn't happen, or that what happened was so minor they should just get over it. In response, they say to themselves, "Why should I even bother? They don't take me seriously." This is why it's important to focus on creating a company culture that encourages conversations about race. As long as the topic stays taboo, it's going to be nearly impossible to address race-related problems in the workplace.

We live together but in different worlds. One of my colleagues told me that he never met a Black person until he was in college and that the vast majority of the people in his professional and social circle since then have been White. He told me that when he went to Ghana, it was an eye-opening experience. Everyone he saw and everyone he met was Black. He was there for weeks and never saw another White person. "The whole time I was conscious of the fact I was different. I'd never felt like that before, and I've never felt like that since. When I was there, I went out of my way to make a friendly impression on everybody. I knew I was different, but I didn't want people to think I was different in a bad way. For many of them, it might have been their first experience with a White man. Maybe I felt like I was representing White people. I didn't want my difference to create any sense of negativity about me."

I couldn't help but smile at my friend's story. That's how many BIPOC around the world feel in the workplace every day. But if you've never had the experience of being surrounded by people but feeling alone because of your race, it's hard to empathize. It's also hard to understand the importance of seeing other people who share your background, as we saw at ANI recently when working with a new company. In our qualitative assessment work, we received two very disparate perspectives on affinity groups in the workplace:

Person 1: My hope is that we can learn that affinity groups are divisive and problematic and are completely unnecessary in our company.

Person 2: My hope is that we can realize the value of affinity groups and finally start giving them the resources they need.

This disconnect is why difficult conversations about race are such an important part of the advocacy process. They help create a common ground from which to initiate change. The more comfortable the people around us are with having these conversations, the more effective our advocacy can be. You can't solve a problem if you can't talk about the problem. Therefore, a major part of advocacy needs to include increasing psychological safety and companywide trust and improving the communication skills of the people within the organization.

Think of the tools that I've given you in this book as a seed. A seed is nothing if it is not planted in fertile soil. Psychological safety and willingness to lean into these conversations comprise the soil necessary for these conversations to germinate within your organization.

Marisa Tatum, director of communications at Strategic Diversity Partners, has found that simply creating opportunities for people of different backgrounds to talk to each other specifically about race-related issues has had significant benefits for improving the company culture and creating more connection between colleagues of different backgrounds. She said, "When I create these spaces for dialogue, I've found that creating commonality is the key. Commonality tends to draw people in. When they can relate to each other it leads to understanding and understanding leads to empathy."[12]

For example, in the summer of 2020 during the height of the Black Lives Matter movement, she was able to connect with a colleague by sharing her fears for her husband, a twelve-year military veteran. Tatum said, "I told him that when my husband is out past a certain time, I still get nervous [despite his military background] because I know he's at a greater risk of being the victim of a police shooting. I could see [my coworker's] realization of how this issue that seems so far away for him, is so personal to me."

We can create commonality through connection whenever we're given the opportunity to engage. "You realize everyone wants the same thing," Tatum notes. "Everyone wants to be healthy and happy, and wants their family to be safe." But these conversations often don't happen organically within organizations, because departments tend to be siloed and people tend to self-segregate. That's why it's so important to create structured opportunities for people to connect, communicate, and learn about one another in a safe environment.

This highlights a problem with many of the current implicit-bias trainings: they actually *inhibit* people's willingness to connect across racial and ethnic lines, working against the creation of the fertile ground necessary to support difficult conversations about race. Traditional implicit-bias trainings are ineffective at best,[13] and, according to some research, they often backfire and make things *worse* at the company.[14] Many trainings inadvertently reinforce previously held biases,[15] creating division and frustration in the workplace,[16] or make it *less* likely for BIPOC employees to advance in the organization.[17]

Traditional bias training also tends to focus on all the ways that people can fail during conversations about race. Psychologist Paula Caligiuri, author of *Build Your Cultural Agility*, believes that focusing so intently on the negative "takes away the exact thing that fosters authentic conversations, which is the desire to connect and be with and communicate with someone who is demographically different," by ramping up the level of fear and trepidation people have regarding these difficult conversations.[18] As a result, people are less likely to try to have difficult conversations, or, for that matter, even interact with people who have backgrounds different from their own. They're too afraid of making a mistake.

Now, this is not to say that we shouldn't be doing bias trainings. We should just be doing them *the right way*. For example, when we do bias trainings at ANI, we focus on three things:

1. Awareness of the science of bias
2. The skills needed to overcome biases
3. The requisite mindset to actually put those skills into action

This approach works because, as Francesca Gino and Katherine Coffman state in the *Harvard Business Review*, "the most effective [bias] training does more than increase awareness of bias and its impact. It teaches attendees to manage their biases, change their behavior, and track their progress.

It gives them information that contradicts stereotypes and allows them to connect with people whose experiences are different from theirs."[19]

This book emphasizes strategies that acknowledge the psychological reality of bias and create techniques to overcome bias in yourself and in others. It also shows how you can navigate conversations in a way that mobilizes biases positively in order to create connection.

Individual conversations do not exist in a vacuum. If organizations want to tackle these critical race-related issues, there needs to be a cultural shift that includes encouraging people to have these difficult conversations while equipping them with the tools to have them at a high level. This is what's needed to create that fertile ground for these conversations to happen in productive and constructive ways.

WHEN ALL ELSE FAILS . . .

Kwame, I've tried everything you've told me, I've used the techniques outlined in your book, and I have brought my leadership team data that shows clear racial and gender disparities. I've been trying to push for change for over a year and the company has done nothing to address racial inequity. They just keep saying no. What can I do?

I'm a diplomacy-first kind of guy. When there's a problem, I always try reaching out to the individual or organization in question first, in order to give them an opportunity to work with me to solve it. However, I understand that tools such as the Compassionate Curiosity framework, empathy, and respectful communication can only go so far. Sometimes, regardless of how well you make your case, people are simply unwilling to change.

In these cases, I suggest using what in negotiation is called *co-opetition*, a blend of cooperation and competition.[20] With this strategy, you continue to use the standard principles of persuasion outlined in this book to try to inspire cooperation, while at the *same time* leveraging more competitive strategies, like lawsuits or boycotts. These are examples of what we described as *negative leverage* earlier in this chapter. With this strategy, you're creating a meaningful incentive for them to consider the gravity of the situation.

If a company's racial issues are significant enough, you may need to enlist assistance from outside of your organization in the form of lawyers or the media. However, keep in mind that this is a method of last resort and should only be used in extreme circumstances. Not surprisingly, once you put more extreme measures into play, it will fundamentally change your relationship with the organization as a whole and the individuals within it. Thus, as you take this step, it's vitally important for you to consider the consequences.

Let's say that you believe that your company discriminated against you because of your race. You might continue negotiating with the company in order to find a solution even while, *at the same time,* you begin working with lawyers to prepare to sue in court *just in case* the company isn't willing to address the problem.

Here's what that can look like in practice. In 2020, fifty-two Black McDonald's franchise owners sued over their claim that they were steered to franchise locations in Black, inner-city, or rural communities over more potentially lucrative locations. According to the lawsuit, the plaintiffs earned, on average, $700,000 less net profit per restaurant than the national average. Soon after the suit was filed, news broke that McDonald's had instituted several ambitious DEI policies and goals. They linked 15 percent of senior executives' bonuses to improving diversity, along with several other notable commitments toward racial equity such as "targeting 35% of U.S. senior management to be from underrepresented groups by 2025."[21] It is likely that the lawsuits created the *negative leverage* necessary to encourage the leadership to prioritize making significant changes—the kind of changes employees had been seeking for a while.

Legal strategies aren't your only option, even if your company isn't taking your concerns seriously. Campaigning to raise awareness, conducting assessments to gather more evidence of racial inequities, going to the media, and using a peaceful protest are all legitimate approaches to getting your voice heard and the inequities you see addressed. As an advocate, you need to find a way to put your finger on the scale to sway the results in your favor. It is not always easy, and the right approach isn't always obvious, but sometimes it is the only option.

DISCUSSION QUESTIONS

- What change do you want to create in your organization?
- What are some barriers you face within your organization as an advocate?
- Think of a time that you tried to advocate in the past. How did it go? Knowing what you know now, what would you do differently?

CHAPTER
EIGHT

THE ROLE OF DIFFICULT CONVERSATIONS IN EQUITY DISCUSSIONS

Generally speaking, people think highly of Dr. Martin Luther King Jr. Today, more than fifty years after his death, he enjoys a favorability rating of 90 percent.[1] However, while he was alive, the majority of Americans saw him as a controversial and unlikeable figure. According to a 1966 Gallup poll, "Americans were nearly twice as likely to have a negative (63%) as positive (33%) opinion of him."[2] Most White Americans saw King as an irritant. From White America's perspective, everything was fine; King was creating problems, not solving them.

When you're advocating for change within your organization, you may be seen as an irritant, too. Difficult conversations can make people uncomfortable, and that discomfort can lead people to blame the irritant, because it seemed as though everything was fine before someone spoke up. People often struggle to see a problem if it's not a problem for them. But the "irritant" of advocacy is the medication necessary to cure the greater ill of racism.

When it comes to change, as we've seen, people often will resist, saying things like, "This isn't the 'right way' to go about doing things." Often, when somebody says the way you're doing something is not the "right" way, it's because the existing power structures are being challenged and they feel threatened. Their criticism often doesn't come with a replacement proposal; it's just meant to tear down yours.

As we wrap up our journey together, I want to leave you with some parting words of encouragement and final thoughts to keep in mind as you put the tools from this book into action.

COLLABORATION OVER COMPETITION

Most people who want to create positive change in their organization want to do so in safe ways. They don't have the privilege to risk losing their job and putting their family at financial risk. They also don't want to risk victimization or abuse. Urging reform can put people in a precarious position because they may need to balance advocating for what they believe is right with not jeopardizing their family's security and their own. Also, if they lose their job, they also lose their opportunity to advocate for change from within.

Yet if you want to be a change agent, you may need to take that risk. It's much easier to drive organizational change from within an organization than from outside of it. But the best way to minimize that risk is a diplomatic approach. That's why this book has focused on giving you the tools you need to blend advocacy and efficacy without jeopardizing your role in the organization. You now understand how to communicate in a way that blends assertiveness with empathy. The strategies you've learned are designed to be effective while respecting the underlying relationship with the person you're communicating with. These conversations *need* to happen, and tools from this book give you the ability to lean into these conversations wholeheartedly and authentically in a way that allows you to be effective, respectful, clear, and direct while deftly avoiding some predictable barriers to success.

The approach we've outlined in this book is not intuitive, but it *is* effective, and we know it's effective because it has been used successfully in all kinds of difficult conversations at the highest level in the business world for the past half-century. This methodology is substantiated by science and validated by thousands of professionals all around the world over their decades of experience.

Old-school negotiation philosophy was driven by competition and aggression, predicated on the false assumption that we're always playing a zero-sum game where more for me means less for you. This toxic approach created worse outcomes for those involved while destroying relationships in the process. Thankfully, the advent of the collaborative model of negotiation changed this. The business leaders who adopted this new model made the transition *because the approach worked*. Lawyers, executives, and leaders recognized that, through creativity and cooperation, they could work together to create more value for everybody at the negotiation table.

There's no need to reinvent the wheel for having difficult conversations about race; we just need to recalibrate our steering. The same methodology can and will work for all such conversations. I know it will because I've seen it firsthand with our clients at ANI. They've been able to improve their ability to have difficult conversations, change company cultures, and create policies and structures within their organizations to promote diversity, equity, and inclusion. In other words, they've been able to Negotiate Real Change.

THE POWER IS IN YOUR HANDS

One of my biggest frustrations in this space is how some well-meaning people focus more on what's wrong than how to make it right. They'll complain about the substantial problems and challenges we face, but rarely offer tangible guidance on *what* you can do about it. This creates feelings of both learned helplessness and apathy.

Remember, you have *significant* influence. But you can't put your success in the hands of others. Pointing the finger at your conversation partner and blaming them for your conversation going poorly is a disempowering position. Yes, it might be their fault, but we likely bear some responsibility, too, by not using an approach that anticipates and overcomes predictable barriers. By focusing on other people and what they are doing wrong in the conversation, we prevent ourselves from seeing what we can do right.

Many people struggle in difficult conversations about race because they approach them as if they live in an ideal world. Yes, in theory, people *should* change their position when they are presented with facts, data, statistics, and evidence. And people *should* adjust their perspective when they are faced with the reality of the inherent contradictions of their perspective. But, as we've seen throughout this book, human psychology does not adhere to our rules for how the world should be. We can't have these conversations in the world as it should be; *we have to have these conversations in the world as it actually is*—with a healthy respect for how the intricacies of the mind impact the way our messages are received.

In the words of Billie Jean King, an incredible advocate for social justice, "Champions adapt and adjust." I want you to be a champion of racial justice and equity in your organization. Are you willing to make the necessary adjustments?

BUILD THE ROSTER

In his 1963 *Letter from Birmingham Jail*, Dr. Martin Luther King Jr. describes the greatest barrier to justice and equity for Black people in America as not "the Ku Klux Klanner, but the white moderate, who is more devoted to 'order' than to justice; who prefers a negative peace which is the absence of tension to a positive peace which is the presence of justice; who constantly says: 'I agree with you in the goal you seek, but I cannot agree with your methods of direct action,' . . . constantly advis[ing] the Negro to wait for a 'more convenient season.'"[3] King recognized that success was impossible without White allies marching alongside him.

Although our society has made progress toward racial equity, there's still a long way to go. And just like in 1963, we need allies to help push things in the right direction. Diversity, equity, and inclusion includes *you*, whoever *you* happen to be. With the skills you learned from this book, you have the opportunity to work together to create a future that works for *all of us*.

In the 2010s, the NBA entered what's been called the era of the "super-team," where the rosters of the most successful teams include multiple all-stars, while teams without the same depth of talent struggle to compete. You want to apply the same approach those winning NBA teams do to DEI efforts within your organization.

In that light, I encourage you to start thinking like a team general manager and always be on the lookout for top talent. Everyone you talk to is a potential recruit as you build your roster of allies. Teams are more effective than individuals; the stronger the team, the more likely you all will be to achieve your goals. Your individual political capital within your organization is limited, but by building a larger team, you avail yourself of much more power.

In part one, we talked about how, for many people, talking about race is incredibly challenging. Many White people, in particular, were raised to believe that talking about race in any capacity is impolite. Furthermore, they may fear saying something wrong and being labeled a racist. As a result, they choose not to engage, which means that some powerful potential allies are sitting on the sidelines out of fear. This hurts the cause of equity because, in order to create a fair, just, equitable, and inclusive society, we need people of *all* races to be allies and advocates.

According to the psychological phenomenon of *diffusion of responsibility,* many good people *won't* take action because they assume that someone else will do what needs to be done.[4] Because of this, when you recruit allies, be clear about the fact that you want and need their assistance.

Let's say you've identified an instance of racial inequity in your workplace. Here are a few questions you can ask after sharing your discovery:

- What do you think about the situation?
- What do you think we could do about it?
- I can't do this alone. What do you think you can do to help?

Then continue to let the Compassionate Curiosity framework guide the way.

You need to encourage and motivate potential allies to engage by helping them recognize that they are a vital component for success. This is especially important when talking with someone who is not directly harmed by the inequity you've identified. Remember, successful civil rights movements require people of all races—and the same will be true at your workplace.

How to Be an Ally

If you're an ally, here's what you can do to best support your superteam:

1. *Consider your strengths.* What are your strengths? Where and how are you positioned within your company that might be useful in driving change? Doing a quick analysis will help you understand how you can use your unique skills and position to maximize the impact of your words and actions.
2. *Identify inequity.* Allyship is easier when there is a clear target. Becoming more aware of inequities in your environment is a necessary first step for determining what change you want to accomplish.
3. *Ask for guidance.* It's important to be humble in approaching an issue of inequity, especially when you are not directly affected. Assume that you're not seeing the whole picture and talk to the people who are most affected by the situation. (*Caveat*: If you are a White person in an all-White space, don't use the difficulty of performing this step as an excuse not to take action.)
4. *Take action.* Allyship is something you do, not a title you have. You've identified a problem and asked for guidance, which means you now have everything you need to take action. If you are unsure of how you can act effectively, return to step one: What are your unique strengths? How are you uniquely positioned to add value? Then decide:
   - How will you take action?
   - *By when* will you take action? (It's important to set a time frame for your action. If there is no set time, it's unlikely you will take any action at all.)

When I was learning to play tennis, my coaches would always tell me, "If you are going to miss, it's better to hit the ball out of bounds than into the net." If you hit the ball into the net, then you never had a chance to get the point; if you hit the ball out of bounds, at least it went over the net. The same is true of allyship. It's better to "miss" actively than passively. Active errors give you the opportunity to learn and correct your mistakes so you can build on your past performance. Don't think of it as failure; think of it as feedback. In the words of the great tennis champion and civil rights leader Arthur Ashe, "Start where you are. Use what you have. Do what you can." That's all we can ask.

MOVE THE NEEDLE IN YOUR OWN WAY

Don't feel as if you have to create sweeping change all at once. Instead, focus on what *you* are trying to accomplish in each conversation you have. Maybe it's shifting the other person's perspective. Maybe it's just getting them to open themselves up to the possibility that there could be another way to see the world. These types of conversations matter. Take advantage of the everyday opportunities to have them.

One of the reasons I burned out the first time I started doing equity work was that I didn't take the time to appreciate small wins. Make your goals attainable and celebrate when you achieve them. A change that might be imperceptible to others can be a monumental win for you.

The tools from this book are designed to be portable and customizable. The strategies you've learned aren't only useful in a workplace setting, or only in talking about race; you can use them in all of your difficult conversations. This also gives you a wider variety of conversations that you can use for practice.

Try to use these tools as frequently as possible, so that they become a part of you, something you do automatically, rather than something you need to think about doing. For me, I look at negotiation not as a skill, but as a life philosophy, and I filter every single human interaction I have through this lens. It helps me to be much more intentional about the way I engage with the people around me. It also helps me keep my skills sharp because every interaction becomes a practice opportunity.

Whatever you do, be true to yourself. I like to keep things fun, light, and approachable in difficult conversations because, as a negotiator and an educator, I've found this helps people feel comfortable lowering their mental barriers, and makes it more likely that they will engage with my message. One of my colleagues who did mediations in the same courthouse I did once said, "I've never heard anyone get people to laugh in mediations, but people are always laughing in yours. I don't know how you do it." That's just what works for me. It makes my mediations smoother, my difficult conversations easier to manage, and the trainings I do more enjoyable, while also helping me achieve my ultimate goals.

I've built this approach from a blend of my understanding of psychology, negotiation strategy, and my authentic personality. I don't want you to read this book and say, "I want to be like Kwame." I want you to read this book and say, "I want to be a better version of myself." I am only a guide. I cannot advise you on the best ways to make changes in your specific environment, nor can I tell you how to best use your talents. You need to take stock of your own personal inventory of badassery, and then pick your own path.

Which of the skill sets and mindsets outlined in this book will work for you? Adopt them and make them your own. I don't expect everybody to agree with 100 percent of the way I approach difficult conversations. If, after reading this book, you start to be more intentional about how you communicate, I will consider that to be a massive win. That's one way I move the needle. You'll find your own.

This book is a starting point that I hope will empower you to go out and make positive change within your workplace, and beyond—in your families and communities. It has presented copious real-world examples of how-tos and how-to-nots, which I know can feel overwhelming at first. You might be feeling as if the challenge of furthering racial equity is insurmountable. It is not. You now have the ability to effect change within your life and surroundings. You can make a difference.

NEGOTIATING A BETTER TOMORROW

None of what I'm asking of you is easy. I know these conversations about race are difficult. Fortunately, your ability to perform in difficult conversations is a skill, not a talent. You can improve. Still, improvement isn't going to happen overnight. It's going to be hard, and you're going to make mistakes. The Compassionate Curiosity framework is not a panacea for the psychological and emotional barriers you'll face, in yourself and others.

Furthermore, the rhetoric in politics today is more vitriolic and divisive than ever. We need to depoliticize the issue of race as much as possible because equity, fairness, and justice shouldn't be partisan issues. They should be American ideals.

My hope is that this book sparks conversations that generate new ideas, solutions to complex problems, and deeper levels of understanding. It's not *my way* or *your way*, it's *our way* and *let's figure out a way to solve these problems together.* The collective is wiser than the individual.

The more we lean in and have these conversations, the more we will learn and the more our confidence in our skills will grow, which will aid our advocacy efforts. My goal is for this book to generate spirited discussions not only about race, but also about *how to talk about* race.

That said, ask yourself: What did you agree with in this book? What did you disagree with? I always tell my staff, "Don't make me feel good, make me better." I am open to and encourage criticism. All I ask is that you use your criticism as an opportunity to spark more conversation on this topic. Let your voice be heard.

Together, we have a unique opportunity to create the kinds of just, equitable, and inclusive workplaces that we all want to see. When you think about what it will take to change the structures and policies within your organization, it can feel daunting, but remember the large changes that organizations underwent during the COVID-19 pandemic: they are in fact capable of significant amounts of change.

In the words of my favorite musician, Bob Marley, "Emancipate yourself from mental slavery / None but ourselves can free our minds." When it comes to what we can do to change our organizations, we're only limited by our imagination. *Anything that doesn't violate a physical law is subject to renegotiation.* If it was made by a human, then it can be changed by a human.

Change often starts with a great question: Why do we do things this way? What if we did them another way? If the answer is, "It's just the way we've always done it," that's not good enough. Especially in older organizations, the rules were negotiated at a time when women and BIPOC did not have a seat at the table. The world has changed, and it's time to renegotiate these rules, norms, policies, and structures in a way that works for *everyone*.

Inclusivity means that people feel comfortable being their true and authentic selves in the workplace. As an organization, we have to create a culture where we all can feel as though we belong. That doesn't happen simply by hiring diverse employees or performing a few trainings. The only way it happens is through true and meaningful structural change that creates not only equity but also opportunities for meaningful connection.

Roger Kelly, the former leader of the KKK, asked Daryl Davis, a Black man, to be his daughter's godfather.[5] Thanks to the meaningful connection the men formed through many difficult conversations about race, they're not just friends, they're family.

Every person in your organization is different and unique. When we take the time to communicate and connect with one another, focusing on our commonalities while acknowledging and accepting our differences, we create opportunities for understanding. We have difficult conversations about race because conflict is an opportunity: an opportunity to connect, grow, solve problems, and create the positive change we want to see.

Remember, the best things in life are on the other side of difficult conversations. Have the courage to lean in, and use these conversations as an opportunity to create the world you want to see.

DISCUSSION QUESTIONS

- What is something you can do to move your company toward racial equity?
- Who are three people in your workplace that you would consider recruiting to become allies? Why do you think they would be good allies, and what is your plan to approach them?
- What is the most surprising thing you have learned while reading this book? How can that previous gap in your knowledge base create an opportunity for future learning?

APPENDIX

THE ADVOCATE'S PLAYBOOK: HANDLING COMMON RACE-RELATED SCENARIOS AT WORK

would be remiss if I didn't briefly discuss how you can use the tools in this book to handle some challenging race-related conversations that come up frequently between coworkers in the workplace. These particular situations are especially challenging because you don't always see them coming; since you don't have time to prepare, it makes it hard to know how to respond. These examples will give you some simple strategies that you can use to navigate similar situations with confidence. And, as always, when you don't know exactly what to say, you can use Compassionate Curiosity to lead the way.

INAPPROPRIATE COMMENTS DURING MEETINGS

Scenario: Someone makes an inappropriate comment in a meeting and it looks like other people are about to join in.

When it comes to meetings, it's important to consider the concept of *persuasive momentum*, or the directional energy generated by an accumulation of comments, statements, or agreements. In negotiation, it's better to start the conversation by talking about points of agreement, rather than points of contention, because it generates positive momentum for the discussion. It's much easier to address more difficult topics when you've had a few successes with smaller topics.

Momentum can go in the opposite direction as well. Sometimes a bad idea gains momentum, and it's hard for people to go in another direction. With race, someone might say something inappropriate, and then another person doubles down on what the first person said, and it continues to roll.

When this happens, you want to stop the growth of that momentum. When a team is gaining momentum in sports, the coach on the opposing team sometimes tries to break that momentum by calling a timeout. The same slow-down approach applies here. Saying something like, "Hey, I'm not comfortable with the direction this conversation is going. Let's circle back and talk about . . ." and then direct an on-topic open-ended question at a specific person to get the conversation headed in a different, more productive direction. Then, after the conversation, you can talk directly to the person who made the inappropriate comment (the calling-in strategy we discussed earlier in the book).

DOUBLE STANDARDS

Scenario: A manager tells you, a Black woman, that your afro is "unprofessional."

YOU: To clarify, you said my hair was unprofessional. Can you help me to understand what it is about my hair that is unprofessional?

THEM: Our company policy requires that all staff and personnel come to work in professional attire which includes clothing, hair, and maintaining proper hygiene. In my opinion, your hair looks a little bit unkempt, and therefore does not meet the required guidelines as outlined by our company policy.

YOU: I don't disagree with the company policy and want to make sure I am maintaining a professional image. Here's the thing, though, when my hair is in an afro, my hair is in its natural state. When it grows, it grows upward. My friend Martha, who's White, has hair that naturally grows downward. Is her hair unprofessional when it's down in its natural state?

THEM: (*slight hesitation*) No . . .

YOU: OK, so let me make sure I'm understanding this correctly. My hair in its natural state is unprofessional, and Martha's hair in her natural state is professional. Is that right?

THEM: (*more hesitation*) Yes . . . Well . . . ummm.

YOU: What I'm having trouble understanding is what makes her natural hair more professional than my natural hair.

If you get to this point of the conversation, it's likely that you will be hit with that awkward silence. Remember, don't rescue the other person; let them feel that awkwardness, as it is a very, very important part of the process.

At this point, your questions may have done enough to persuade the person without further effort on your part—in this case, that the person was wrong to call your afro unprofessional. If not, this is where you would transition to engaging in joint problem solving to address the situation with specific solutions that are fair, equitable, and respectful. For example, you could ask, "Considering what we've discussed thus far, what changes can we make to the current policy in order to make it more inclusive?" This question begins the shift toward future-focused problem solving where you invite the other person to be part of the solution rather than seeing them as part of the problem.

ASSUMPTIONS BASED ON IMPLICIT RACIAL BIASES

Scenario: You're talking with a colleague, and they mention their hope that a BIPOC football player doesn't embarrass his team by using broken English during a press conference.

YOU: What makes you think he would speak with broken English?

THEM (REALIZING THE PROBLEM): Ooh, this is one of those times where I was being insensitive, wasn't it?

(You nod.)

THEM: Noted. Thank you for that. I'm sorry.

What the other person said was most certainly a microaggression. Did they mean it to be offensive? No. Was it offensive? Yes. Asking them to explain the unspoken assumptions behind their statement allows you to hold them accountable and shift their thinking while still being mindful of the relationship. Remember, you're doing this for both your sake and theirs. It helps you because it decreases the likelihood of having to endure further offensive comments, and it helps them because they learn where they fell short and what they need to do to improve.

It's helpful to recognize, in situations like this, that the other person may not even know that what they are saying is a problem until it gets brought to their attention. Oftentimes a simple question—for example, "What makes you think X?"—is enough to get the person to become more aware. Here, once the issue was gently brought to their attention, the other person did the right thing by apologizing and, presumably, adjusting their thinking for the future. They did not over-apologize, which can be awkward and diminishes the interaction by turning the apology into a request for reassurance.

Not only is this approach more likely to avoid their feeling defensive and doubling down on their original statement; it also grows the relationship. They will appreciate the grace you extended by not vilifying them for their mistake, and you have the opportunity to see and appreciate their humble adjustment.

It's important, when using this approach, not to dwell on what happened. Acknowledge it fully in the moment, then move on.

INAPPROPRIATE JOKES

| *Scenario*: Someone made a racially offensive joke.

In standup comedy, a certain level of dark or irreverent humor is acceptable. Comedy in the workplace is different. With standup comedy, *everybody agreed to go there and hear jokes*. At your job, *everybody agreed to go there and work*. You and your coworkers aren't there to hear other people's hot takes. People who attend a comedy show usually know the comedian they've chosen to see, and therefore know what kind of humor they're going to hear. They can also leave the show if they don't like what they hear. Leaving work isn't an option.

We can think about a joke as a kind of negotiation. In a negotiation, if you want to make a deal, you make an offer. If the other side likes it, they accept it. When someone tells a joke, they are offering humor, and the people who hear the joke accept that humor by laughing or smiling. A favorable response to the joke is a tacit endorsement of the joke's contents.

In the case of humor that you found to be offensive, you can never accept the offer of the joke because it encourages similar jokes in the future, and signals acceptance of the ideas behind it. Your first step is to reject the offer of the joke by not laughing or giving even a polite smile.

For your second step, you have a couple of options. One is to directly and succinctly demonstrate that you don't condone that type of humor by saying, "Not cool" or, "Not okay."

Your other option is to highlight the problem with the joke by asking them to explain it. Play ignorant and ask, "I don't get it. Can you please explain it to me?" Inappropriate humor is usually inappropriate because its unspoken premise—the implicit understanding required for the punchline to make sense—is offensive. The reason why the premise is problematic is usually because it reinforces racism in some fashion. So when you ask the other person to explain the joke, the only way they can do so is by stating the racist belief that allows the joke to make sense. Simply asking the question is usually enough for them to get the message because it forces them to wrestle with the problematic portions of their humor. And since they are the one who needs to explain, it makes the process much easier for you. You don't need to lecture them about the problematic nature of what was said; they come to the conclusion themselves.

FLAGRANT RACISTS

| *Scenario*: Your manager is openly hostile to BIPOC in your department.

This situation is a little trickier, because the problem isn't an individual comment or joke; it's a pattern of behavior that is clearly motivated by bias. Accordingly, just having a conversation with that person is unlikely to be enough to change their behavior. Trying to do so is often a waste of your time.

Think about it like triage. As much as medical professionals want to help everybody, in emergency situations they have to prioritize the people who have the best chance of survival, and that can mean letting go of people who are too far gone to help. While you don't want to write people off too soon, sometimes, in these difficult conversations about race, you realize that the person you're talking to is too far gone to change.

Even when you consider the story of Daryl Davis and the KKK members he converted, remember, with some members, changing their minds took him *years*. In situations like this, you have to consider the return on investment. You could have hundreds of individual productive conversations with hundreds of different people in the same time it takes you to convert one person who is very resistant to change.

Does that mean that, when it comes to these people, you never have difficult conversations? Well, not exactly. Here's an example of what a strategic approach to this kind of challenge could look like.

A coaching client I worked with was dealing with a manager who, after over ten years in the position, had never promoted a person of color despite many having worked for him. Other people had spoken to him directly about it without success, so we determined that the best thing to do was to "remove the obstacle" by having the difficult conversation with company leadership rather than with the manager himself.

We put together a negotiation strategy where my client first generated some positive persuasive momentum by talking to the manager's peers—other managers on the same level—about my client's concerns, to make them aware of the situation and collect further evidence to substantiate them. Once my client had gathered more support from their own team and from the other higher-level managers, my client then laid out their case to the director, stating their claims and providing documentation. The director resisted, but my client made it clear that this was a problem that needed to be solved, so if the director was uncomfortable addressing the situation, my client would take the problem to the CEO of the entire company (the director's boss). My client felt confident in this strategy because of the CEO's recent public statement about diversity, equity, and inclusion.

When faced with the proposition of my client going over their head, the director had a change of heart and removed the problematic manager. As a result, the entire culture of that division changed. It was like a weight was lifted off of everybody's shoulders. And once that manager was removed, multiple BIPOC were promoted in the division.

ENDNOTES

INTRODUCTION

1. Centers for Disease Control and Prevention, "FastStats—Health of Black or African American Population," April 14, 2021, https://www.cdc.gov/nchs/fastats/black-health.htm.
2. Yascha Mounk, "Americans Dislike PC Culture," *The Atlantic*, October 10, 2018, https://www.theatlantic.com/ideas/archive/2018/10/large-majorities-dislike-political-correctness/572581/.
3. Gina Belli, "Here's How Many Years You'll Spend at Work in Your Lifetime," *PayScale*, October 1, 2018, https://www.payscale.com/career-advice/heres-how-many-years-youll-spend-work-in-your-lifetime/.
4. Belli, "Here's How Many Years."

CHAPTER ONE

1. Marcus E. Raichle and Debra A. Gusnard, "Appraising the Brain's Energy Budget," *PNAS* 99, no. 16 (2002): 10237–39, https://doi.org/10.1073/pnas.172399499.
2. Jing Li, Wen Wang, Jing Yu, and Liqi Zhu, "Young Children's Development of Fairness Preference," *Frontiers in Psychology* 7 (2016): 1274, https://dx.doi.org/10.3389%2Ffpsyg.2016.01274.
3. Jaak Panksepp, *Affective Neuroscience: The Foundations of Human and Animal Emotions* (New York: Oxford University Press, 1998).

4. Sylvia Ann Hewlett, "Too Many People of Color Feel Uncomfortable at Work," *Harvard Business Review,* October 18, 2012. https://hbr.org/2012/10/too-many-people-of-color-feel.

CHAPTER TWO

1. US Department of Commerce, Economics and Statistics Administration, Bureau of the Census, 1990.

2. L. Comas-Díaz, G. N. Hall, and H. A. Neville. 2019. "Racial Trauma: Theory, Research, and Healing: Introduction to the Special Issue." *American Psychologist* 74 (1): 1–5.

3. Jennifer Warner, "Bad Memories Easier to Remember," *WebMD*, August 29, 2007, https://www.webmd.com/brain/news/20070829/bad-memories-easier-to-remember.

4. James Clear (@JamesClear), "Every action you take is a vote for the type of person you wish to become. No single instance will transform your beliefs, but as the votes build up, so does the evidence of your identity," Twitter, October 7, 2018, 12:35 A.M. https://twitter.com/jamesclear/status/1048612840615997441?lang=en.

5. Kwame Christian and Katherine Knapke, *Finding Confidence in Conflict: How to Negotiate Anything and Live Your Best Life* (Columbus, Ohio: American Negotiation Institute LLC, 2020).

6. Carol Dweck, *Mindset: The New Psychology of Success* (New York: Penguin Random House, 2006, 2016).

7. Ijemoa Oluo, *So You Want to Talk About Race* (New York: Seal Press, 2018).

8. Kendra Cherry, "What Is the Negativity Bias?", *Very Well Mind*, April 29, 2020, https://www.verywellmind.com/negative-bias-4589618.

9. Kimberly Holland, "Cognitive Behavioral Therapy for Depression," last modified December 13, 2021, https://www.healthline.com/health/depression/cognitive-behavioral-therapy.

10. Good Therapy, "Exposure Therapy," last modified July 3, 2015, https://www.goodtherapy.org/learn-about-therapy/types/exposure-therapy.

CHAPTER THREE

1. Kamal Gulati, "Here's Why Having a Brain Means You Have Bias," July 22, 2020, https://neuroleadership.com/your-brain-at-work/unconscious-bias-in -brain.

2. Science Daily, "Why Expensive Wine Appears to Taste Better: It's the Price Tag," August 14, 2017. www.sciencedaily.com/releases/2017/08 /170814092949.htm.

3. Greg Norman, "Georgetown Law Fires Professor Who Made 'Reprehensible Statements' About Black Students on Viral Video," *Fox News*, March 11, 2021, https://www.foxnews.com/us/georgetown-law-fires-professor -reprehensible-statements-black-students-viral-vide0.

4. Derek Schaedig, "Self-Fulfilling Prophecy and the Pygmalion Effect," *Simply Psychology*, August 24, 2020, https://www.simplypsychology.org /self-fulfilling-prophecy.html.

5. PsycholoGenie, "Some Examples of Fundamental Attribution Error Which We Make Daily," accessed January 22, 2022, https://psychologenie .com/fundamental-attribution-error-examples.

6. Saul McLeod, "Fundamental Attribution Error," *Simply Psychology*, 2018, accessed February 5, 2022, https://www.simplypsychology.org /fundamental-attribution.html.

7. Kwame Christian, "Finding Confidence in Conflict," filmed at TedxDayton, video, 11:27, https://www.ted.com/talks/kwame_christian_finding _confidence_in_conflict.

8. Southern Poverty Law Center, "Ku Klux Klan," n.d., accessed February 6, 2022, www.splcenter.org/fighting-hate/extremist-files/ideology/ku-klux -klan.

9. Dwane Brown, "How One Man Convinced 200 Ku Klux Klan Members to Give Up Their Robes," *NPR*, August 20, 2017, https://www.npr.org/2017 /08/20/544861933/how-one-man-convinced-200-ku-klux-klan-members -to-give-up-their-robes.

10. Iqra Noor, "Confirmation Bias," *Simple Psychology*, June 10, 2020, https:// www.simplypsychology.org/confirmation-bias.html.

11. Stephen Johnson, "Fake Martial Arts: The Psychology Behind 'No-Touch' Knockouts," *Big Think*, February 4, 2020, https://bigthink.com/thinking /fake-martial-arts/.

12. Ibram X. Kendi, "The Heartbreak of Racism Is Denial," January 13, 2018, *The New York Times*. https://www.nytimes.com/2018/01/13/opinion /sunday/heartbeat-of-racism-denial.html.

13. Robin Stern, "I've Counseled Hundreds of Victims of Gaslighting. Here's How to Spot If You're Being Gaslighted," *Vox*, December 19, 2018, https:// www.vox.com/first-person/2018/12/19/18140830/gaslighting-relationships -politics-explained.

14. Peace Corps, "The Blind Men and the Elephant," n.d., accessed June 24, 2021, www.peacecorps.gov/educators/resources/story-blind-men-and -elephant.

15. Chip Heath and Dan Heath, "The Curse of Knowledge," *Harvard Business Review*, December 2006, https://hbr.org/2006/12/the-curse-of-knowledge.

16. Daniel Effron, Benoit Monin, and Dale T. Miller, "The Unhealthy Road Not Taken: Licensing Indulgence by Exaggerating Counterfactual Sins," *Journal of Experimental Social Psychology* 49, no. 3 (2013) 573–78, https:// www.researchgate.net/publication/256752581_The_unhealthy_road_not _taken_Licensing_indulgence_by_exaggerating_counterfactual_sins.

17. Benoit Monin and Dale T. Miller, "Moral Credentials and the Expression of Prejudice," *Journal of Personality and Social Psychology* 81, no. 1 (2001): 33–43.

18. *American Psychological Association Dictionary of Psychology*, s.v. "Catharsis," accessed February 6, 2022, https://dictionary.apa.org/catharsis.

19. Ashley Brown, "Catharsis Psychology," *Better Help,* updated December 23, 2021, https://www.betterhelp.com/advice/psychologists/16-examples -of-catharsis-psychology/.

20. Lamm Claus and Jasminka Majdandžić, "The Role of Shared Neural Activators, Mirror Neurons, and Morality in Empathy: A Critical Comment," *Neuroscience Researcher* 90, no. 15 (2015): 15–24.

21. William J. Hall, Mimi V. Chapman, Kent M. Lee, Yesenia M. Merino, Tainayah W. Thomas, B. Keith Payne, Eugenia Eng, Steven H. Day, and Tamera Coyne-Beasley, "Implicit Racial/Ethnic Bias Among Health Care

Professionals and Its Influence on Health Care Outcomes: A Systematic Review," *American Journal of Public Health* 105, no. 12 (2015): e60–e76, 10.2105/AJPH.2015.302903.

CHAPTER FOUR

1. Mark Davis, interview with Kwame Christian, *Negotiate Anything*, podcast audio, 2020, https://podcasts.apple.com/cy/podcast/using-cultural-intelligence-to-be-effective-negotiator/id1101679010?i=1000484588313.

2. P. Christopher Earey and Elaine Mosakowski, "Cultural Intelligence," *Harvard Business Review*, October 1, 2004, https://store.hbr.org/product/cultural-intelligence/R0410J.

3. Matthew Thompson, "Five Reasons Why People Code Switch," April 13, 2013, *NPR Code-Switch*, https://www.npr.org/sections/codeswitch/2013/04/13/177126294/five-reasons-why-people-code-switch.

4. Earey and Mosakowski, "Cultural Intelligence."

5. Jason Christie, "How to Exceed Market Expectations," interview with Kwame Christian, 2021, *Negotiate Anything*, podcast audio, https://play.acast.com/s/negotiate-anything/howtoexceedmarketexpectationswithjasonchristie.

6. Adam L. Alter and Daniel M. Oppenheimer, "Uniting the Tribes of Fluency to Form a Metacognitive Nation," *Personality and Social Psychology Review*, July 28, 2009, https://doi.org/10.1177/1088868309341564.

7. Frank Luntz, *Words That Work: It's Not What You Say, It's What People Hear* (New York: Hachette Books, 2015).

8. Centers for Disease Control and Prevention, "Infant Mortality," last modified September 8, 2021, https://www.cdc.gov/reproductivehealth/maternalinfanthealth/infantmortality.htm.

9. Peter Boghossian, *How to Have Impossible Conversations: A Very Practical Guide* (New York: Lifelong Books, 2019).

10. American Negotiation Institute, "How to Have Difficult Conversations About Race Prep Guide," n.d., www.americannegotiationinstitute.com/guide.

11. Stewart Diamond, *Getting More: How You Can Negotiate to Succeed in Work and Life* (New York: Penguin Random House, 2018).

CHAPTER FIVE

1. V. Rajmohan and E. Mohandas, 2007. "The Limbic System." *Indian Journal of Psychiatry* 49, no. 2(2007): 132–39, http://doi.org/10.4103/0019-5545.33264.

2. Adele Diamond, "Want to Optimize Executive Functions and Academic Outcomes?" *Minnesota Symposium on Child Psychology* 37 (2014): 205–32, https://www.ncbi.nlm.nih.gov/pmc/articles/PMC4210770/.

3. Amy F. T. Arnsten, "Stress Signaling Pathways That Impair Prefrontal Cortex Structure and Function," *Nature Reviews Neuroscience* 10, no. 6 (2010): 410–22, 10.1038/nrn2648.

4. Lisa J. Burklund, David Creswell, Michael Irwin, and Matthew Lieberman, "The Common and Distinct Neural Bases of Affect Labeling and Reappraisal in Healthy Adults," *Frontiers in Psychology*, March 14, 2014, https://www.frontiersin.org/articles/10.3389/fpsyg.2014.00221/full.

5. Lisa J. Burkland, Michelle G. Craske, Shelley E. Taylor, and Matthew D. Lieberman, "Altered Emotion Regulation Capacity in Social Phobia as a Function of Comorbidity," *Social Cognitive and Affective Neuroscience* 10, no. 2 (2014): 199–208, 10.1093/scan/nsu058.

6. Daniel Siegel, "Name It to Tame It," Dalai Lama Center for Peace and Education, December 8, 2014, video, 4:20, https://www.youtube.com/watch?v=ZcDLzppD4Jc.

7. Matthew Tull, "Secondary Emotions and Post-Traumatic Stress Disorder," *Very Well Mind*, updated April 26, 2020, https://www.verywellmind.com/secondary-emotions-2797387.

8. Harvard Health Publishing, "Writing About Emotions May Ease Stress and Trauma," October 11, 2011, https://www.health.harvard.edu/healthbeat/writing-about-emotions-may-ease-stress-and-trauma.

9. University of Rochester Medical Center, "Journaling for Mental Health," n.d., https://www.urmc.rochester.edu/encyclopedia/content.aspx?ContentID=4552&ContentTypeID=1.

10. Phillip Houston, *Spy the Lie: Former CIA Officers Teach You How to Detect Deception* (New York: St. Martin's Press, 20130).

11. Program on Negotiation Staff, "Dear Negotiation Coach: Responding (or Not) to an Ultimatum in Negotiation," Program on Negotiation Daily Blog, Harvard Law School, January 19, 2021, https://www.pon.harvard

.edu/daily/dispute-resolution/dear-negotiation-coach-responding-or-not-to-an-ultimatum-nb.

12. Chris Voss and Tahl Raz, *Never Split the Difference: Negotiating as If Your Life Depended on It* (New York: HarperCollins, 2016).

13. Kwame Christian, interview with Becki Saltzman, "How to Use Curiosity for Powerful Persuasion," *Negotiate Anything*, podcast audio, 2018, https://americannegotiationinstitute.com/how-to-use-curiosity-for-powerful-persuasion-with-becki-saltzman/.

14. Kwame Christian, interview with Chris Voss, "How to Negotiate Like an FBI Agent," 2016.

15. Helene Haker, "Mirror Neuron Activity During Contagious Yawning—An fMRI Study," *Brain Imaging Behavior* 7, no. 1 (2013): 28–34, 10.1007/s11682-012-9189-9.

16. J. M. Kilner and R. M. Lemon, "What We Know Currently About Mirror Neurons," *Current Biology* 23, no. 23 (2013): R1057–R1062, 10.1016/j.cub.2013.10.051.

17. J. A. C. J. Bastiaansen, M. Thioux, and C. Keysers, "Evidence for Mirror Systems in Emotions," *Philosophical Transactions of the Royal Society of London B: Biological Sciences* 364, no. 1528 (2009): 2391–404. 10.1098/rstb.2009.0058.

18. *Merriam-Webster*, s.v. "Buy-In (*n.*)," accessed February 6, 2022, https://www.merriam-webster.com/dictionary/buy-in.

19. R. Fisher and D. Shapiro, *Beyond Reason* (New York: Penguin Books, 2006).

CHAPTER SIX

1. Cornell Law School Legal Information Institute, "Affirmative Action," accessed February 7, 2022, https://www.law.cornell.edu/wex/affirmative_action.

2. United States Census Bureau, "Quick Facts," accessed February 7, 2022, https://www.census.gov/quickfacts/fact/table/US/RHI825219.

3. Center for the Study of Hate & Extremism, "Fact Sheet: Anti-Asian Prejudice March 2021," accessed January 13, 2022, https://www.csusb.edu/sites/default/files/FACT%20SHEET-%20Anti-Asian%20Hate%202020%20rev%203.21.21.pdf.

4. Kerry Patterson, Joseph Grenny, Ron McMillan, and Al Switzler, *Crucial*

Conversations: Tools for Talking When Stakes Are High, 2nd ed. (New York: McGraw-Hill, 2011).

5. Brené Brown, *Daring Greatly: How the Courage to Be Vulnerable Transforms the Way We Live, Love, Parent and Lead* (London: Portfolio Penguin, 2013).

6. Brené Brown, "Companion Worksheet: *I Thought It Was Just Me (but It Isn't): Making the Journey from "What Will People Think?" to "I Am Enough,"* 2019, accessed January 13, 2022, https://brenebrown.com/wp -content/uploads/2021/09/ITIWJM_Worksheet.pdf.

7. You might be saying, "Kwame, I don't care how the other person feels about being called racist; I'm going to tell it like it is. I'm going to call a spade a spade and they just have to deal with it." I respect that. And if using potentially triggering words during the conversation is aligned with your ultimate goals, use them. I just want to make sure that you're aware, *before* you use the word, of what is likely to happen as a result.

8. Ibram X. Kendi, *How to Be an Antiracist* (New York: One World, 2019).

9. Daniel Kahneman, *Thinking, Fast and Slow* (New York: Farrar, Straus and Giroux, 2011).

10. Stewart Diamond, "Emotion: The Enemy of Negotiation," *Wharton Magazine,* Spring 2011, https://magazine.wharton.upenn.edu/issues/spring-2011 /emotion-the-enemy-of-negotiation/.

11. Laurel Beatty Blunt, "How to Improve Communication Skills," interview with Kwame Christian, *Negotiate Anything,* podcast audio, 2020, https:// podcasts.apple.com/us/podcast/how-to-improve-communication-skills -with-judge-laurel/id1101679010?i=1000554700273.

12. National Human Genome Research Institute, "New Genome Comparison Finds Chimps, Humans Very Similar at the DNA Level," *NIH News,* August 31, 2005, https://www.genome.gov/15515096/2005-release-new -genome-comparison-finds-chimps-humans-very-similar-at-dna-level.

CHAPTER SEVEN

1. Mursion, "Allyship and Advocacy: What Is the Best Way to Offer Active Support in the Workplace?", March 23, 2021, https://www.mursion.com /articles/allyship-and-advocacy/.

2. Kendi, *How to be An Antiracist.*

3. James Clear, *Atomic Habits: An Easy and Proven Way to Build Good Habits* (New York: Penguin Random House, 2018).

4. Kendi, *How to Be an Antiracist*.

5. Frank Newport, "In U.S., 87% Approve of Black-White Marriage, vs. 4% in 1958," Gallup, July 25, 2013, https://news.gallup.com/poll/163697/approve -marriage-blacks-whites.aspx.

6. Safiya Charles and Byron Dobson, "Historically Black Colleges Fight for Survival, Reopening Amid Coronavirus Pandemic," *USA Today*, June 9, 2020, https://www.usatoday.com/story/news/education/2020/06/09/coronavirus -hbcu-colleges-fall-semester-2020/5286165002/.

7. G. Richard Shell, *Bargaining for Advantage: Negotiation Strategies for Reasonable People* (New York: Penguin Books, 2006).

8. Shell, *Bargaining for Advantage*, 6.

9. This is another example of egocentric persuasion.

10. Cornell Law School Legal Information Institute, "Preponderance of the Evidence," accessed June 24, 2021, https://www.law.cornell.edu/wex /preponderance_of_the_evidence.

11. NBBJ, "Design Justice," accessed January 14, 2022, http://www.nbbj.com /about/design-justice/.

12. Kwame Christian, interview with Marisa Tatum, 2021.

13. Tiffany Green, "The Problem with Implicit Bias Training," *Scientific American*, August 28, 2020, https://www.scientificamerican.com/article /the-problem-with-implicit-bias-training/.

14. Francesa Gino and Katherine Coffman, "Unconscious Bias Training That Works," *Harvard Business Review*, September–October 2021, https://hbr .org/2021/09/unconscious-bias-training-that-works.

15. Michelle M. Duguid and Melissa C. Thomas-Hunt, "Condoning Stereotyping? How Awareness of Stereotyping Prevalence Impacts Expression of Stereotypes," *Journal of Applied Psychology*, 100, no. 2 (2015): 343–59, 10.1037/a0037908.

16. Green, *The Problem*, 21.

17. Gino and Coffman, *Unconscious Bias*, 21.

18. Paula Caligiuri, interview with Kwame Christian, *Negotiate Anything*, podcast audio, 2021, https://podcasts.apple.com/us/podcast/how-to-build-your -cultural-agility-with-paula-caligiuri/id1101679010?i=1000532363850.

19. Gino and Coffman, *Unconscious Bias*, 21.

20. Adam Brandenburger and Barry Nalebuff, "The Rules of Co-opetition," *Harvard Business Review,* January–February 2021, https://hbr.org/2021/01/the-rules-of-co-opetition.

21. Crayton Harrison and Anne Riley Moffat, "McDonald's Ties Executive Pay to Diversity, Releases Data," *Bloomberg,* February 18, 2021, https://www.bloomberg.com/news/articles/2021-02-18/mcdonald-s-ties-executive-pay-to-diversity-goals-releases-data.

CHAPTER EIGHT

1. Nicolas Boyon, "A 90% Favorability Rating for Martin Luther King Jr. on His 90th Birthday," Ipsos, January 18, 2019, https://www.ipsos.com/en-us/news-polls/90-favorability-rating-martin-luther-king-jr-2019-01-18.

2. Jeffrey M. Jones, "Americans Divided on Whether King's Dream Has Been Realized," Gallup, August 26, 2011, https://news.gallup.com/poll/149201/americans-divided-whether-king-dream-realized.aspx.

3. Martin Luther King Jr., "Letter from Birmingham Jail [King, Jr.]," African Studies Center, University of Pennsylvania, n.d. (source date April 16, 1963), https://www.africa.upenn.edu/Articles_Gen/Letter_Birmingham.html.

4. *Britannica,* s.v. "Diffusion of Responsibility," accessed January 1, 2022, https://www.britannica.com/topic/bystander-effect/Diffusion-of-responsibility.

5. Jeffrey Fleishman, "A Black Quixotic Quest to Quell the Racism of the KKK, One Robe at a Time," *Los Angeles Times,* October 8, 2016, https://www.latimes.com/entertainment/movies/la-ca-film-accidental-courtesy-20161205-story.html.

INDEX

A

abilities, conflict to improve, 32
absolutes, 172–173
academic terminology, 98
acceptance, code switching for, 85
accountability, 166–167
achievable goals, 193
acknowledging emotions, 43, 114,
    118–119, 123, 126–133, 149
action(s)
    acknowledging another's, 55
    advocacy and, 181
    by allies, 206
    collective, 7–8
    as factor in control, 78
active errors, 207
active preparation, 79
adaptation, 183, 204
adjustment, 204
advantage, perspective influenced by,
    22
advocates, 181–200
    allies vs., 181
    bending of rules by, 189–192
    better vs. perfect solutions for, 194
    conditions for positive change
        created by, 194–198
    co-opetition by, 198–199

defined, 181–182
leverage for, 184–187
maximizing impact by, 182–184
mental health and, 187–189
Negotiate Real Change Model for,
    192–193
Advocate's Playbook, 213–219
Affective Neuroscience (Panksepp),
    23
affect labeling, 119–120
affinity, mutual, 71
affinity bias, 70–71
affinity groups, 195–196
African Americans. *see* Black
    individuals
age, of conversational partner, 8
aggression, 117, 129, 203
agreement
    finding opportunities for, 131
    pre-negotiations for terms of, 191
    respect vs., 164
allyship, 181, 204–207
American Negotiation Institute (ANI)
    on active preparation, 79
    addressing race-related complaints
        at, 170–172
    on affinity groups, 195–196
    bias training at, 197

ANI *(continued)*
　DEI trainings and strategic
　　consulting at, 64, 176
　guiding principle of, 1, 2
　infant mortality messaging from,
　　99–100
American Psychological Association,
　68
amygdala, 115
Angelou, Maya, 39
ANI. *see* American Negotiation
　Institute
apathy, 117, 203
apologizing, 216
appeals to emotion, 174–175
appreciation, 143
"appropriate" tone, 140
Arbery, Ahmaud, 4
arguments, semantic, 154–159
arrogance, 107–108
Asian Americans, 23, 159. *see also*
　BIPOC individuals
asking questions. *see also* questions
　conversational patterns and, 163
　as conversational strategy, 100–106
　to create change, 183–184
aspirational statements, 90, 98
assessments, conducting, 199
associations, unconscious, 48
assumptions
　identifying, 65
　and implicit racial bias, 216–217
　questioning, 50–51
Atomic Habits (Clear), 182
attribution bias, 51–58
authenticity, 23
avoidance
　and defensiveness, 216
　due to previous conversations,
　　41–42
　for energy conservation, 18
　and negative leverage, 185
awareness
　of biases, 197

　of race as factor in identity, 38
awkward, feeling, 5, 215

B

baby steps, in conversations, 63–64
baggage, emotional, 28–31
Bargaining for Advantage (Shell), 184
baselines, for mutual understanding, 63
Bastiaansen, J. A. C. J., 138
Beatty Blunt, Laurel, 174
beliefs
　challenging another's, 129
　confirmation bias to support, 58
　control over others', 78
　as factor in identity, 59
　self-limiting, 35
　shared core, 71
　strongly-held vs. new, 175
　and topics at hand, 176
　willingness to challenge your, 108
belittled, feeling, 29
benefit of doubt, 54–55
best, assuming the, 54
better, 23, 194
bias(es)
　affinity, 70–71
　attribution, 51–58
　confirmation, 58–62, 175
　defined, 47
　Dunning-Kruger effect, 61
　implicit, 47–51, 197, 216–217
　ingroup and outgroup, 69–70
　negativity, 40
　overcoming, 82, 197
　positive, 82
　responding based on, 102
bias checks, 50–51
binary thinking, 33–34
BIPOC individuals, 7
　comfort of, in workplace, 23
　positions of, in workplace, 22
　questions about equity of, 64
　race in identity of, 36–37
　tone policing of, 139–140

birth, conditions of, 78
Black individuals. *see also* BIPOC
   individuals
  authenticity in workplace for, 23
  inconsistent healthcare for, 71
  infant mortality of, 3, 99–100
blame, 65, 203–204
"The Blind Men and the Elephant"
   (folktale), 61
blind spots, 38
body language, 136
Boston Housing Authority, 93
boundaries, setting, 21
box breathing, 125
brain, energy use by, 18–19
brainstorming sessions, 141–142
British government, 185
Brown, Brené, 164–166
Brown v. Board of Education, 183
Build Your Cultural Agility (Caligiuri),
   197
burden of proof, 190
burnout, 187–189
"but," using word, 137

C
Caligiuri, Paula, 197
calling in, 95–97
calling out, 95
campaigning, 199
canceled, fear of being, 6, 39, 167
caring
  about colleagues, 19–21
  about fairness, 19
  about progress, 19, 22–23
  in workplaces, 18
catharsis, 68
CBT (cognitive behavioral therapy), 42
Center for the Study of Hate and
   Extremism, 159
certainty, of facts, 190
challenging questions, 183–184
chantable phrases, 98
Christian, Kwame, 28, 52, 53, 113

Christie, Jason, 85–86
clarity
  asking "why" to gain, 121
  Compassionate Curiosity
   framework to gain, 113, 122
  defining terms for, 157
  of messaging, 98
  and use of "racism" label, 170
Clear, James, 35, 182
closed-ended questions, 106
code switching, 84–86, 140
Coffman, Katherine, 197–198
cognitive behavioral therapy (CBT), 42
collaboration, 89–93
  in equity discussions, 202–203
  framing conversation for combat
   vs., 89–91
  for problem solving, 141 (*see also*
   joint problem solving)
  situation + impact + invitation
   formula for, 91–93
collaborative model of negotiation, 203
colleagues, caring about, 19–21
collective action, 7–8
color blindness, 19–20
combat
  conflict vs., 31, 34
  framing for collaboration vs., 89–91
comfort, 23, 93, 139
comments, inappropriate, 214
common ground, finding, 131, 196–197
communication. *see also* persuasive
   communication
  about needed support, 21
  effective, 8, 24
  impact of psychology on, 46
  levels of, 86–89, 129
communication skills, building, 196
company culture, 194–198, 219
compassion
  other-directed (*see* other-directed
   compassion)
  self-directed (*see* self-directed
   compassion)

Compassionate Curiosity framework,
9–11, 113–152, 174
acknowledging/validating emotions
in, 118–119, 123, 126–133, 149
applying steps of, 122–124,
147–151
effectiveness of, 114–116
getting curious with compassion in,
119–123, 133–143, 149
joint problem solving in, 122, 123,
141–143
for people with stuck emotions,
143–147
self-directed compassion in,
116–125
and tips keep cool, 124–125
using, with others, 125–151
competition, 198–199, 203
complacency, 66–67
comprehension checks, 109
compromise, negotiation vs., 81
confidence, 43
action and, 35
confirmation bias and, 60–61
as factor in success, 56
locus of control and, 34
positive cycle of, 35
too much, 107–108
confirmation bias, 58–62, 175
conflict, overcoming, 2, 24–25, 31–33
confrontational people, 55
connecting with others
by acknowledging and validating
emotions, 130
by code-switching, 84
confidence about, 56–58
to overcome conflict, 31
consistent standards, 106
continuous news cycles, 187–189
contradicting standards, 106
control
acknowledging limits of, 78–79
Compassionate Curiosity
framework for gaining, 151

emotional, 173–174
impact of emotions on, 118
locus of, 34
note taking to regain, 125
shame and loss of, 166
conversational detours, 104
conversational frames, collaborative,
89–93
conversational strategies, 77–112
asking questions, 100–106
calling in, 95–97
and core values/mistreatment,
80–82
establishing collaborative
conversational frames, 89–93
expressing empathy, 110–111
holding people to their own
standards, 106–107
and humility, 107–110
and levels of communications,
86–89
in one-on-one conversations, 93–95
and simplicity/fluency of messages,
97–99
speaking to the heart, 99–100
trust building, 82–86
Cooper, Amy, 41
cooperation, 198–199
co-opetition, 198–199
COQUAL, 23
core beliefs, shared, 71
core instincts, 23
core values, 80–82
Cornell Law School, 154
correcting people, 87–88
counterpoints, 173, 175
COVID-19 pandemic, 3
CQ (cultural intelligence), 84
Cravener, Veronica, 32
criticism, 83, 190, 202, 209
Crucial Conversations (Patterson et.
al), 163
cultural dialects, 84
cultural intelligence (CQ), 84

cultural momentum, 185
culture
    company, 194–198, 219
    workplace, 23
curiosity, 114, 119–123, 133–143, 149
current perspectives, core values and, 81
current strongly-held beliefs, new vs., 175
Curry, Steph, 56
curse of knowledge, 62–64

D
data, using, 99–100, 109
Davis, Daryl, 56–57, 101, 163–164, 210, 218
Davis, Mark, 84
decision making
    impact of biases on, 47
    impact of emotions on, 100
    standards for, 191–192
Decker, Mark, 40–41, 168
defensiveness
    accountability and, 167
    avoidance and, 216
    call-ins to reduce, 96
    in conversations, 106
definitions of terms, establishing, 154–159
DEI (diversity, equity, and inclusion) training, 2
denial, racism and, 60
depoliticizing issues of race, 209
Design Justice plan, 193
dialects, cultural, 84
Diamond, Stuart, 106
difficult conversations, avoiding, 3–4
diffusion of responsibility, 205
diminished, feeling, 165
disagreements, 32, 45–46
discomfort, emotional, 119, 141, 153.
    see also uncomfortable, feeling
disconnection, fear of, 164
discrimination, racial, 27–28

dismissed, feeling, 165
disrespect, 163–164
diversity, equity, and inclusion (DEI) training, 2
dodging questions, 161–162
double standards, 214–215
doubt, benefit of the, 54–55
Dunning-Kruger effect, 61
Dweck, Carol, 35

E
egocentric persuasion, 159–163
emotion(s)
    acknowledging, 43, 114, 118–119, 123, 126–133, 149
    addressing, 132–133
    appeals to, 174–175
    in Compassionate Curiosity framework, 118–119, 123, 126–133
    discomfort with, 119, 141, 153
    dismissing another's, 46
    emotional challenges vs., 115
    impact of biases on, 73
    managing your, 115–125
    negative, 28–31, 68
    of others, as situations outside of your control, 78
    in persuasion, 99–100
    psychology of, 52–53, 116
    reconciling logic/reason with, 122
    secondary, 120
    underestimating, 173–175
    validation of, 67–68, 118–119, 123, 126–133, 149
    writing to process, 125
emotional baggage, 28–31
emotional challenges, 115
emotional contagion, 138–139
emotional one-upping, 68
emotional payment, 171
emotional regulation, 115–125
emotional relief, 122
emotional self, 117–118

empathetic inquiry, 133
empathetic persuasion, 159–163
empathy
    code-switching to increase, 84
    emotional struggles and lack of, 117
    and great pain-off, 69–71
    intentional, 69–71, 88, 111
    in level one communication, 88
    psychological, 69–71, 83
    for undeserving people, 110–111
energy, conserving, 18–19, 79
energy shield masters, 58–59
engagement
    as factor in conversations, 9
    lecturing and, 108–110
    and situation + impact + invitation
        formula, 96, 169
entrenchment, 129
epistemological approach, 100–106
equity
    barriers to, 22
    conflict to promote, 32
    impact of moral licensing on, 66
    just world fallacy and, 64
Equity at Work (COQUAL), 23
equity discussions, 201–211
    collaboration in, 202–203
    finding allies, 204–207
    individualizing framework,
        207–208
    and negotiating better tomorrow,
        209–210
    personal power for, 203–204
evidence, using, 189–192
expansion of perspective, 61–62
expectation setting, 21, 31, 144
explanations, 66, 217–218
exposure therapy, 42

F
facts
    confirmation bias and interpreting,
        59
    in conversations, 189–192

feelings vs., 128
    naked, 91–92
failure, manifesting, 56
fairness
    caring about, 19, 21–22
    just world fallacy and, 64
fear
    avoiding difficult conversations due
        to, 5, 6
    of being canceled, 6, 39, 167
    of disconnection, 164
    of making mistakes, 197
    of offending others, 39, 83–84
    of things not understood, 57
    winning mindset to overcome,
        41–44
feelings, facts vs., 128. see also
    emotion(s)
fiction, helpful vs. unhelpful, 54, 56
Finding Confidence in Conflict
    (Christian), 28, 54, 113
"Finding Confidence in Conflict"
    (TED Talk), 52, 113
Fisher, Roger, 143
fixed mindset, 35–36
flagrant racism, 218–219
flipping the script, 65–66
Florida A&M University, 183
Floyd, George, 3, 4, 186, 188
fluency of messages, 97–99
follow-up conversations, 33
"fragile," calling conversation partner,
    172
"frequently," use of term, 173
friends, 8, 39
fundamental attribution error, 51–54
funnel technique, 135
future-focused problem solving,
    145–147, 215

G
gains, acknowledging, 67
Gallup Poll, 201
Gandhi, Mohandas, 185

gaps in understanding, 102
gaslighting, 60
"The Genetic Code of Beliefs,"
    175–177
Georgetown Law, 49
Getting More (Diamond), 106
Gino, Francesa, 197–198
goals
    attainable, 207
    conversational, 9, 78
    setting massive, 184
    SMART, 193
good intentions, acknowledging, 171
great pain-off, 67–73
groups, affinity, 195–196
growth mindset, 35–36
guidance, asking for, 206
guilt, shame vs., 165

H
Harvard Business Review, 197
Harvard University, 129, 143
healthy conditions for conversations,
    194–198
heart, speaking to the, 99–100
helpful fiction, 54
helplessness, learned, 203
hope-based strategy, 10, 183
hostility, 117
"how" questions, 134
"How to Have Difficult Conversations
    About Race" (virtual town hall), 4
Human Genome Project, 175
humble, being, 107–110
humiliated, feeling, 29
humor, 146n*, 208, 217
hypothetical questions, 142, 184

I
identity
    belief as factor in, 59
    as factor in conversations, 45
    race as factor in, 20, 36–37
ignorance, 37–38, 110

impact, 92, 182–184
implicit bias, 47–51, 197, 216–217
inappropriate comments and jokes,
    214, 217–218
inclusivity, 8, 22, 23, 210
India, societal leverage in, 185
Indigenous individuals. *see* BIPOC
    individuals
individualizing frameworks, in equity
    discussions, 207–208
inequalities, data about racial,
    99–100
inequity, identifying, 206
infant mortality, 3, 99–100
influence, gaining, 110
"infrequently," use of term, 173
ingroup bias, 69–70, 83
ingroups, 34
instincts, 23
insufficient evidence, 190
intellectual rigidity, 81
intent, positive, 54–55, 83, 144
intentional empathy, 69–71, 88, 111
interactions, before difficult
    conversations, 83
internal narratives, 34–36
interpretations, negative, 51–52
interracial marriages, 183
introspection, 50–51
invalidation, 68, 137
invitation (situation + impact +
    invitation formula), 92–93
irritants, advocates as, 201–202
issue, focusing on one, 94

J
Jenkins, Din, 93
job loss, 39, 167
Jobs.com, 20
joint problem solving, 114, 122, 123,
    141–143, 150–151
jokes, inappropriate, 217–218
judgment, withholding, 55
just world fallacy, 64–66

K

Kahneman, Daniel, 48n*
Kelly, Roger, 57, 101, 163–164, 210
Kendi, Ibram X., 170
Keysers, Christian, 138
King, Billie Jean, 204
King, Martin Luther, Jr., 171, 183,
    201, 204
Kirwan Institute for the Study of Race
    and Ethnicity, 3
K.I.S.S. method, 98
KKK. *see* Ku Klux Klan
knowledge
    curse of, 62–64
    gaps in, 154 (*see also* gaps in
        understanding)
Ku Klux Klan (KKK), 56–57, 101,
    163–164, 210, 218

L

labeling
    affect, 119–120
    people as racists, 6, 30, 39,
        168–170
languages
    and code switching, 84
    speaking different, 154–159
Latinx individuals, 23, 71. *see also*
    BIPOC individuals
laughing, at inappropriate jokes, 217
learned helplessness, 203
learning, about yourself and others,
    31, 87, 108
lecturing, 108–110
Legal Information Institute, 154
legal strategies, after negotiations,
    198–199
Letter From Birmingham Jail (King),
    204
level one communication, 86–88, 129
level two communication, 86, 89
leverage
    from legal strategies, 198–199
    need-based, 184

negative, 198–199
    for positive change, 184–187
    power vs., 184–186
"likely," use of term, 173
limbic system, 115
LinkedIn, 4, 11
listening
    conversation patterns and, 136
    effective, 117
    nonjudgmental, 87–88
    in one-on-one conversations, 93
    to show respect, 164
    talking vs., 43, 151
    validating vs., 130
listening sessions, 43
locus of control, 34
logic, reconciling emotions with, 122
lowering your voice, 139
Luttrell, Andrew, 175

M

macroaggressions, 71
Malhotra, Deepak, 129
Malhotra, Nandini, 189
mantras, 125
Marley, Bob, 209
marriage, interracial, 183
McDonald's, 199
measurable goals, 193
meetings, inappropriate comments
    during, 214
mental health, 28, 187–189
metrics, specific and objective, 193
microaggressions, 6, 71, 216
micro-negotiations, 33, 64
milestones, manageable, 34
mimicry, 85
mindset
    control over, 78
    fixed, 35–36
    growth, 35–36
    winning (*see* winning mindset)
Mindset (Dweck), 35
minimizing racism, 59–60

minimum effective dose, of news, 188–189

mirroring, 134–135

mirror neurons, 138–139

Mirza, Zabeen, 20

mistakes, 153–178
  disrespecting people or their perspectives, 163–164
  fear of making, 197
  relying on egocentric persuasion, 159–163
  speaking different languages, 154–159
  trying to change how another thinks about everything, 175–177
  underestimating emotions, 173–175
  using absolutes, 172–173
  using shame-based strategies, 164–172
  winning mindset about, 38–41

mistreatment, accepting, 80–82

mockery, 85

momentum
  cultural, 185
  persuasive, 214

Moms at Work podcast, 20

moral change, 183

morality, 45, 175

moral licensing, 66–67

moving against shame, 166

moving away from shame, 165

moving toward shame, 165–166

Mursion, 181

mutual affinity, 71

mutual understanding, 97

N

naked facts, 91–92

narratives, internal, 34–36

NBBJ firm, 192–193

need(s)
  failing to see others', 160
  helping others understand our, 21

leverage based on, 184

negative emotions, 28–31, 68

negative interpretations, 51–52

negative leverage, 185, 186, 198–199

negativity
  in conversational patterns, 43
  from emotional baggage, 28–31
  focusing on, 197
  writing to process, 125

negativity bias, 40

Negotiate Anything (podcast), 86, 174, 175

Negotiate Like YOU M.A.T.T.E.R. (Zung), 81

Negotiate Real Change (podcast), 192

Negotiate Real Change Model, 192–193

Negotiating Genius (Malhotra), 129

Negotiating the Impossible (Malhotra), 129

negotiation(s)
  defining, 81
  to ensure better future, 209–210
  jokes as, 217
  micro-, 33, 64
  old-school philosophy for, 203
  pre-, 191
  for real change, 192–193
  with yourself, 117–118

negotiation skills, 4, 24

neurons, mirror, 138–139

Never Split the Difference (Voss), 134

news cycles, continuous, 187–189

new strongly-held beliefs, current vs., 175

nonjudgmental listening, 87–88

note taking, 125

O

offending others, 6, 39–41, 83–84, 216

"often," use of term, 173

old-school negotiation philosophy, 203

one-on-one conversations, 93–95, 97

one-upping, emotional, 68
open-ended questions, 43, 101–106,
    133
openness, in one-on-one
    conversations, 93
opinions, control of others', 78
opportunity-based thinking, 31–32
organizational change, 202
ostracized, being, 39
other-directed compassion
    acknowledging/validating emotions
        for, 126–133
    getting curious with, 133–143
    in joint problem solving, 141–143
outcome-orientated, being, 11
outgroup bias, 69–70
outgroups, 34
over-apologizing, 216

P
pace of speech, 136
pack mentality, 93
pain-offs, 67–72
pains, focusing on current, 67
Panksepp, Jack, 23
past events, 78, 145–147
Patterson, Kerry, 163
pausing, before responding, 174
people of color. *see* BIPOC individuals
perception
    impact of implicit bias on, 47–48
    psychology and, 46, 52–53
perfect solutions, 194
performance, implicit bias and, 49
personal power, 34–36, 203–204
personal responsibility, advocacy as,
    187
perspective(s)
    core values and current, 81
    disrespecting another's, 163–164
    diversity of, 20
    expanding, 38, 61–62, 100–106,
        176
    and perception of fairness, 22

questions to expand, 38, 100–106,
    176
sharing, 87, 134
trying to change another's, 175–177
understanding another's, 33, 108
persuasive communication, 3
    ability of, 56–58
    code-switching for, 84
    egocentric vs. empathic persuasion,
        88, 159–163
    emotions in, 99–100
    K.I.S.S. method for, 98
    in level two communication, 89
    leverage and, 185
    psychology of, 116
    trust and, 83
persuasive momentum, 214
PFC. *see* prefrontal cortex
planning conversations, 78
poise, 32
policy change, 182–183
polite smiles, after inappropriate jokes,
    217
positive bias, 82
positive change, 7–8, 181–200
    bending rules for, 189–192
    calling in for, 95–96
    conflict management for, 24, 31
    co-opetition for, 198–199
    creating conditions for, 194–198
    effective communication for, 24
    focusing on better for, 194
    leverage for, 184–187
    maximizing impact for, 182–184
    mental health and, 187–189
    negotiating real change for, 24,
        192–193
    policy change for, 182–183
Positive Cycle of Confidence, 35
positive intent, 54–55, 83, 144
positive interactions, before difficult
    conversations, 83
positive leverage, 185, 186
positive reinforcement, 142–143

positive self-talk, 125
positive statements, 90
positive tone, 138–139
power
    implicit bias by people in, 48
    leverage vs., 184–186
    personal, 34–36, 203–204
preference, relying on, 47
prefrontal cortex (PFC), 115, 116, 119
pre-negotiations, 191
preparation, for discussions, 79
preponderance of evidence, 190–191
proactive, being, 10
"the problem is" phrase, 137–138
problem solving
    conflict as opportunity for, 32
    future-focused, 145–147
    inability/unwillingness to move
        toward, 144
    joint, 114, 122, 123, 141–143,
        150–151
processing fluency, 97–99
progress, 19
proof, burden of, 190
psychological barriers, 45–73
    attribution bias, 51–58
    confirmation bias, 58–62, 175
    of conversation partners, 82
    and curse of knowledge, 62–64
    and the great pain-off, 67–73
    implicit bias, 47–51, 197, 216–217
    and just world fallacy, 64–66
    and moral licensing, 66–67
psychological empathy, 69–71, 83
psychological entrenchment, 129
public shaming, 95
pushing conversation forward, 145

Q
questions
    closed-ended, 106
    Compassionate Curiosity
        framework for, 133–136
    dodging, 161–162

    hypothetical, 142, 184
    to inspire change, 210
    open-ended, 43, 101–106, 133
    radical/challenging, 183–184
    as strategy for conversations,
        100–106
question softeners, 103

R
race
    as factor in every conversation,
        36–38
    as situation outside of your control,
        78
race, talking about, 17–25
    and conflict as part of progress,
        24–25
    to express care for colleagues,
        19–21
    for fairness, 21–22
    hesitancy about, 5
    for progress, 22–23
    and race as factor in conversation,
        36–38
    risks of, 38–39
race-based stress, 28
race card, pulling the, 39
race-related scenarios, in workplace,
    213–219
racial discrimination, 27–28
racial gaslighting, 60
racial inequalities, data on, 99–100
"racialized outcomes" term, 169
"racially inequitable impact" phrase,
    169
racial trauma, 28, 141
racist(s)
    being labeled a, 6, 30, 39, 168–170
    as trigger word, 168–172
    in workplaces, 218–219
radical questions, 183–184
"rarely," use of term, 173
reason, reconciling emotions with, 122
redemptive approach, 167

reflexive rejection
    asking questions to reduce, 101
    call-ins to reduce, 96
    and confirmation bias, 60–62
    defensiveness and, 167
    trust and, 83
reinforcement, positive, 142–143
rejection
    in disagreements, 45–46
    feeling, 27–28
    reflexive (*see* reflexive rejection)
relevant goals, 193
religious upbringing, 78
repetition of messages, 98–99, 136
resistance, 91, 183, 190
respect
    in conversations, 183–184
    in level one communication, 87
    in negotiations, 81–82
    for people and their perspectives,
        163–164
responsibility, 187, 204, 205
risks, of talking about race, 38–39
Robbins, Tony, 67
rules, bending, 189–192

S
Saltzman, Becki, 134
script, flipping the, 65–66
secondary emotions, 120
seeking instinct, 23
self-advocacy, 20–21
self-awareness, 50–51
self-confidence, 40
self-directed compassion, 40, 116–125,
    122
    acknowledging/validating emotions
        in, 118–119, 123
    applying steps for, 122–124
    getting curious with, 119–123
    joint problem solving for, 122, 123
    negotiations with yourself and,
        117–118
self-forgiveness, 40

self-fulfilling prophecies, 49, 53–54
self-limiting beliefs, 35
self-regulation, 174
self-talk, positive, 125
selves
    bring whole, to work, 8
    emotional and strategic, 117–118
semantic arguments, 154–159
sentence softeners, 134
seven core instincts, 23
70–30 rule, 129
shame, 95, 165–166
shame-based strategies, 117, 164–172,
    166
Shapiro, Dan, 143
Shell, G. Richard, 184
short messaging, 98
shutting down, 117
silence, 102
similarities, pointing out, 70–71
simplicity, of message, 97–99, 151
situation (situation + impact +
    invitation formula), 91–92, 148,
    169
situation + impact + invitation
    formula, 91–96
skepticism, 190
skill building, 2, 32, 36, 197
SMART goals, 193
smiling, after inappropriate jokes, 217
socialization, with friends, 8
societal leverage, 185, 186
socioeconomic status, 78
solutions. *see also* problem solving
    brainstorming sessions to find,
        141–142
    perfect, 194
speaking, listening vs, 43
specificity, 159, 193
speech, pace of, 139
Stalin, Joseph, 99
stalled conversation, 145
standards
    for decision making, 191–192